Australian Biographical Monographs

19

Australian Biographical Monographs

Series Editor: Scott Prasser

Previous Volumes

Annabelle Rankin	Peter Sekuless
Robert (Bob) Hawke	Mike Steketee
John Curtin	David Lee
Jack Lang	David Clune
Leonie Kramer	Damien Freeman
Margaret Guilfoyle	Anne Henderson
William McKell	David Clune
Neville Bonner	Sean Jacobs
George Reid	Luke Walker
Robert Askin	Paul Loughnan
John Grey Gorton	Paul Williams
Stanley Melbourne Bruce	David Lee
Robert Menzies	Scott Prasser
Neville Wran	David Clune
Lindsay Thompson	William Westerman
Johannes Bjelke-Petersen	Bruce Kingston
Harold Holt	Tom Frame
Joseph Lyons	Kevin Andrews

Australian Biographical Monographs

19

Joseph Cook

Zachary Gorman

Connor Court Publishing

Australian Biographical Monographs 19
Joseph Cook by Zachary Gorman
Published in 2023 by Connor Court Publishing Pty Ltd

Connor Court Publishing Pty Ltd
PO Box 7257
Redland Bay QLD 4165
sales@connorcourt.com
www.connorcourt.com

Printed in Australia

ISBN: 9781-922-815-507

Front Cover Photograph: National Library of Australia, Public domain.

I like to think of Australia as the land of the better chance

Joseph Cook, 1918

Series overview

Connor Court's *Australian Biographical Series* on past leading Australian political leaders and other important figures seeks to provide an overview for those who are unfamiliar with the subject and to highlight the person's particular importance, controversies, and contributions to Australia's progress.

The monographs are scholarly rather than academic in focus, placing emphasis on a clear narrative, but with careful attention to referencing to ensure views expressed are supported by appropriate sources and evidence.

The Series was initiated because of the decline in the study of Australian history at our schools and universities. Consequently, there has been a lack of knowledge or, even worse, distorted views, of some of Australia's leading historical figures who deserve to be remembered, better understood for their achievements, and, as each volume also highlights, their flaws.

Clearly, Joseph Cook, our sixth prime minister, is one figure whom many would hardly know but whose brief term as Prime Minister from 1913-14 belies his contributions to Australian government and his own personal achievements. Zachary Gorman in this thoroughly researched monograph ranging from parliamentary debates to contemporary reports, brings Joseph Cook to life. And what a life it was.

Gorman traces Cook's modest but well-grounded early life in England, through to his membership of the emerging Australian Labor Party, representation in the New South Wales Legislative Assembly, and movement on clear principles to non-Labor forces, being elected to the new Commonwealth Parliament, and eventually becoming Prime Minister.

But Cook's career did not end when his government fell from office in 1914 following Australia's first double-dissolution election caused by the Labor Party's Senate obstructionism. Cook went on to become Leader of the Opposition then helped develop with former Labor prime minister, "Billy" Hughes, a new political party – the Nationalist Party which held office from 1917-1929. Cook was de facto Deputy Prime Minister, served as Minister of the Navy and then Treasurer until his retirement in 1921. He was then appointed as Australia's third High Commissioner to the United Kingdom.

This new monograph is not just about Cook's political career, interesting and important as it was. Rather, Zachary Gorman's real achievement is much more. Through excepts of Cook's speeches, reliance on contemporary sources, and coverage of his policies and actions, he has highlighted Cook's principles of independence, self-reliance, individual effort and responsibility and opposition to external pressures all anchored in a strong Christian faith. These were the principles that led Cook away from the Labor

Party as it operated then, and as it operates now. These are principles Liberal leaders today might well consider as they consider their future.

Zachary Gorman has done the *Australian Biographical Series* a service in this account of a great Australian whose achievements and principles are worth being reminded about in these increasingly uncertain times.

■ Scott Prasser

Introduction

Joseph Cook is one of Australia's least remembered prime ministers. Due to another famous figure in Australian history sharing his last name, he has not even had the traditional privilege of having a federal parliamentary seat named after him (though retroactively the seat is now taken to represent both figures). Likewise, if someone were to stumble across the tiny ACT suburb of Cook on the bottom edge of Belconnen, they would likely be surprised to find the famous and now somewhat controversial captain sharing a commemorative sign with a political leader.

To the extent that Joseph Cook is remembered at all, it is as the first in a line of Labor 'rats', those prime ministers who were once a member of the party but who came to lead a non-Labor government. He has received two stand-alone biographies, one John Murdoch's PhD thesis from the 1960s belatedly published as a book in 1996, and another written by G. Bebbington, someone associated with Cook's English hometown who had only limited access to Australian sources; while more recently, Cook has also featured prominently in David Kemp's *A Democratic Nation: Identity, Freedom and Equality in Australia 1901–1925*. The former is generally regarded as the most authoritative account, and it portrays Cook as a model of political inconsistency, shifting his views from radical to conservative over the years, "floating as if a cork on a lifeboat after a particularly unpleasant storm".[1]

But there is another Cook that this monograph seeks to reveal. That is of a self-made man, a true autodidact, whose views broadened as his knowledge grew. His eventual strong support for individual liberty and economic liberalism was intimately associated with how his own story proved that in Australia there was great social mobility and people deserved the freedom to strive and to succeed. It was that Cook, the tireless pit boy who pulled himself up by the bootstraps through hard work and dedication, who became the first federal leader of the Australian centre-right to win a majority in his own right, setting a precedent for what Australian liberalism has meant ever since. His story reveals the how and the why of the emergence of the Australian party system and the philosophical lines of cleavage which continue to define us.

The Pit Boy

Joseph Cooke (as his name was originally spelt) was born on 7 December 1860 in the village of Silverdale, Staffordshire. The place was named after the silver birch which once covered the whole valley in which the town was situated, but by the time Cooke was born much of the area had been denuded of trees in the name of material progress and economic exploitation. Silverdale was after all a "child of the new industrial age", defined by a series of coal mines and the associated industry which at a time when transportation remained prohibitively expensive tended to be carried out in close proximality.[2] With all this available work, the village was booming, more than doubling its population from approximately 2000 people in 1851 to 4,464 in 1861; though the residents themselves remained generally poor and at times quite desperate.

There was one businessman who controlled the town's assorted mines, mills, forges and ironworks, Mr. Stanier of the Silverdale Mining Company. However, the "butty" system meant that individual coal faces were leased out to managers who were personally responsible for seeing that enough coal was mined each day. One such manager was Joseph's father William Cooke, who, though he was hardly well off, embodied aspirational values and was determined to improve his lot in life through perspiration and study. Indeed, during Joseph's youth the family would move houses twice as a sign of their increasing status, though all their residences remained modest and were plagued by rats who bred near the local brook which ran brown from colliery waste water.

William was married to Margaret, née Fletcher, and the two were a model of a close and loving relationship. They took up traditional roles, with William tending to be the disciplinarian and Margaret having a more sweet and comforting nature. Joseph was the second of their seven children, though he essentially functioned as the eldest for the firstborn Sarah would tragically pass away at age six. The boys and the girls each had one room to share, they generally had hand-me down clothes, and only owned one pair of shoes each (but even that was something of a luxury as many of the village's children went barefoot). All the Cooke children who grew to adulthood would go on to have successful careers, a significant testament to the values, positive example and above all self-belief provided by their parents, who insisted that success would come to those who were deserving of it.

These values, which amounted to an empowering vision of the "Protestant work ethic", were partly attributable to the family's Methodism, and from a young age Joseph was instilled with a strong religious conviction which would stay with him throughout his life. Despite not being affiliated with the established church, Joseph was nevertheless sent to the local Church of England School, St. Luke's, which was attached to the parish's house of worship. The school was grossly overcrowded, often filled with smoke from the coal fired stoves that were used for heating and featured elevated windows which were purposefully designed so that children would not be tempted to look out of them and so get distracted.

At a young age Joseph was expected to do a large number of chores and errands, even for neighbours, and at just nine years old he left school to begin working in the mines as a pit boy. Duties included moving wagons of coal, oiling and greasing machinery, and attending to pit ponies – introductory toil which served as an introduction to the even harder labours that were gradually heaped on as boys matured. Cook was blessed with a temporary respite from this fate by the passing of the *Education Act 1870*, which set up a system of local school boards which were able to levy rates and decide if they wanted to make schooling compulsory. This was part of a range of liberal reforms of the Gladstone era, which aimed to foster opportunity for those with the talent and ambition to progress.

Joseph thus returned to St. Luke's with a new sense of perspective that made him a more attentive student, but it was not long before he resumed working in the mines. He was already back at work at the time his employment was made an absolute necessity by virtue of a family tragedy. At 7.30am on 8 April 1873 William was "repairing rails in the dip when a full wagon coming down, came upon him with such force as to bring it to a standstill and tore up some of the rails", which is how the *Potteries Examiner* reported the accident which took William's life at age 39.[3] Such accidents were not uncommon to the harsh existence of a Silverdale miner, and Joseph's younger brother Albert would later meet the same fate when a piece of coal fell down a deep mineshaft and struck him on the head. William was buried with a gravestone that epitomised the family's emphasis that life was about hard work: "Blessed are the dead which die in the Lord for they rest from their labours".

At just twelve years old, Joseph thus became his family's primary breadwinner, a responsibility he came to embrace and which saw him develop an early sense of manhood. He grew strong with a straight and proud back from physically and metaphorically shouldering his burdens, giving him a commanding presence which was reinforced by his piercing blue eyes. The endurance of this healthy posture reflected the fact that he was lucky enough to escape the mines before their conditions could do too much lasting damage to his health (though he did later suffer from a severe bout of rheumatism which may have been related).

That he escaped was Cook's own doing, as he became determined to embark upon a path of self-improvement. Borrowing books from the local chapel he would sit alone in his lunch-break and read by pit lamp. He would also chalk on pit tubs to improve his writing, spelling and arithmetic, and when he got home he would study by candlelight into the early hours of the morning. Later in life when journalist Malcolm Ellis asked Cook about his experiences as a coalminer, he replied with a wry smile that it was "an occupation for a philosopher".[4]

All of this was reinforced and partly inspired by Joseph's Methodism. He was initially associated with the Primitive Methodists who were intimately connected to the working class, functioned in a highly democratic manner, and encouraged self-improvement through education. Crucially, the Methodists rejected determinism and stressed individual agency, a view that would be reinforced by one of Joseph's favourite authors, the American Ralph Waldo Emerson.[5] Since all men and women were equal in the sight of God, Cooke believed that they should be equal in the eyes of the law, but he saw charity as potentially degrading and in line with Gladstonian liberalism was more concerned about removing barriers and abolishing privilege rather than using the state as a paternal benefactor.

Preaching from the age of 16, Joseph became drawn to the New Connexion Methodists under the tutelage of the Reverend James Mellor. Cooke joined the Mutual Improvement Society and was offered the chance to study at the New Connexion College at Ranmoor to become a minister, but he had to turn this down on account of his family commitments. Preaching would inform Joseph's early style as a speaker, and for the rest of his life he was prone to use exaggerated hand gestures, such as slamming his fist into his palm to emphasise a point.

At the age of 18 Cooke joined the Silverdale Liberal Club and began to hone his debating skills. Though he had a love of reading which he attributed to being born in Dr. Johnson's County, Cooke had neither the time nor inclination for most ordinary leisure activities. He was a proselytising teetotaller (the demon drink being his favourite topic to speak on as a preacher) and was generally uninterested in sport, though unusually for the time he was fond of swimming and would later advocate that it become a compulsory part of schooling in coastal areas.

With all the time he invested in self-improvement, Cooke became a respected figure in the mining community and attained the position of checkweighman, whose responsibility it was to assess the pay due to each miner based on the amount of coal they had mined. He also became involved in the local trade union, which was active in responding to wages pressure caused by the economic downturn of the early 1880s. The union engaged in what proved to be fruitless strikes, and Cooke learned from bitter experience how this bargaining method could easily backfire and hurt those it was intended to help. In the end Cooke had to leave Silverdale and found temporary work cleaning and maintaining engines for the North Staffordshire Railway Company.

Around the same time, Cooke met and fell in love with Mary Turner, a young school teacher and the daughter of a respected coke burner. The two made quite the pair, partly modelled on the strong bond of Cooke's own parents. Her teaching skills helped to reinforce Joseph's self-education, as she would correct his arithmetic and read aloud for him to practice his shorthand (a skill he meticulously developed, and which would later serve him well as a parliamentarian as he relentlessly confronted opponents with accurate quotations of what they had actually said).

Mary would be a constant source of support and advice throughout Cooke's life, maintaining a relaxing home in which he could withdraw from the world. They would be married 62 years and produce nine children, who would be raised with that same mixture of love and discipline that Cooke knew from his own childhood.

It was Mary and the economic downturn which ultimately inspired Cooke to make the move to Australia. She had a brother who lived in Lithgow New South Wales, a mining town that bore strong similarities to Silverdale, and he would write letters attesting to the constant work and good wages which could be found there. Cooke's younger siblings had by this stage largely grown up, and "having brought up one family under very hard conditions" he was determined not to have to repeat the process.[6] He sailed out of Plymouth through thick fog on Christmas Day 1885, leaving behind Mary who was pregnant with their first child, who would be named George Sydney to mark their new and hopeful beginning.

The Labor Representative

Joseph Cook arrived in Australia on 12 February 1886. According to biographer John Murdoch this was the occasion when Cook dropped the "e" from his last name to symbolise the new beginning, though others date this to his earlier experiences as a Methodist preacher.[7]

Arriving at the height of summer, the weather must have been a severe shock to the Englishman, but otherwise Cook fitted in quite naturally. He made his way to Lithgow in the Central Tablelands of New South Wales, and soon proved his brother-in-law's optimism to be well founded by finding a job as a skilled miner (allegedly breaking a strike to do so) and quickly re-attaining his old position as checkweighman. He began building a timber house on Macaulay Street and saving for the arrival of his family, and even started preaching for the local Primitive Methodist congregation.

Progress was so rapid that Mary and George were able to arrive in January 1887. This acted as a spur to further acts of self-improvement, as Cook looked to potentially become a journalist or an accountant. He briefly worked for the *Lithgow Enterprise and Australian Land Nationaliser*, but the paper went bankrupt. Unperturbed, Cook soon had part-time jobs auditing the books of the *Lithgow Mercury* and the local council. In the mines, he became union lodge president, pushing for the introduction of new techniques to make mining safer such as the water cartridge which had helped to vastly reduce gas explosions and mining-related deaths in North Staffordshire.[8] Cook also arranged conferences with mine owners on pay and conditions, and by 1889 he was auditing the paysheets of every pit in Lithgow.

It was Cook's interest in both journalism and unionism, and his quite organic emergence as a leader of men, which prompted him to begin engaging with local politics. In 1887 he was involved in a demonstration calling for the introduction of an 8-hour day; in 1888 he supported a proposal to restrict Chinese immigration, fought to stop a mine being built under the Lithgow water reserve, and seconded a motion to incorporate Lithgow as a municipality; while in 1889 he lobbied the Minister for Works to help provide work for unemployed members of the local district.[9] While all of these issues reflected the particular interests of the local miners, they could not be said to represent a broader philosophy on government. This is something that would take Cook a while to develop, and as a self-educated man he prided himself on taking the time to weigh up both sides of an argument, and also being willing to change his views as and when his knowledge grew.

This is typified by his approach to the tariff issue, which at the time was considered all-important. Indeed, what were arguably the first real political parties in New South Wales politics emerged at the 1887 election where the candidates divided themselves into Free Traders (led by the political veteran Henry Parkes) and Protectionists. Initially, Cook was predisposed to support tariff protection and even served as Secretary of the Lithgow Protection Union; a position likely informed by the fact that the economic woes of Silverdale were partly caused by import competition.

However, by 1890 Cook eschewed his previous affiliation and publicly declared that the worker would get no benefit from tariffs.[10]

The catalyst for the change of heart was likely Henry George, the famous American social reformer who visited Lithgow in 1890 and who was influential in both Free Trade circles and the early Labor movement.[11] George's 1879 book *Progress and Poverty* sought to explain why the great material progress the United States had experienced during the 19th century had failed to dramatically raise living standards for ordinary people. His conclusion was that most of the newly created wealth had been syphoned off by landowners, who increased the price of land faster than wealth was produced, and that this process was particularly acute in rapidly industrialising cities.

George's utopian solution was the implementation of a "single tax" on the unimproved value of land.[12] This tax was meant to replace all other forms of taxation and would attack the institutionalised wealth of property owners while leaving others free from the burden of the costs of government. The fact that the tax was on the "unimproved" value was meant to encourage people to continue to develop their land while punishing those who lived off the "unearned increment" that was derived through ownership and inflation rather than work. The tax was therefore meant to curb land speculation and tax city properties, whose value was derived from their location, more than rural farm properties whose value was derived from what was produced on them. George wanted to use the tax to "appropriate rent"; hence land taxation was a roundabout way of achieving a pseudo nationalisation of land.

At face value, George's philosophy sounds socialist and revolutionary; however, there were elements of the 'single tax' which attracted some liberals. These included having a somewhat restrained overall level of taxation and therefore scope for government and encouraging free enterprise and individual initiative by never penalising the improvement of land or any form of profit creation that was not based on land. George was not an opponent of capitalism and wanted to "increase the earnings of capital" and "afford free scope to human powers".[13] It is notable that Cook would later take offence at a political opponent who tried to lump in 'land taxers and single taxers' with 'socialists and anarchists'; Cook was in the former camp but not the latter.[14]

On the issue of free trade, George attacked tariffs as something that taxed consumers and decreased standards of living, particularly for the poor. They benefited a few privileged monopolistic vested interests, while failing to tangibly raise wages in the way that advocates claimed. This was largely because protectionist theory involved dividing up a limited pie rather than increasing its overall size. Protecting one industry raised the price of materials used for other businesses, hurting overall economic growth, which was a large part of what was needed to provide new jobs and increased wages. Borrowing from Adam Smith's arguments in *The Wealth of Nations*, George pointed out that:

> Trade is not invasion. It does not involve aggression on one side and resistance on the other, but mutual consent and gratification... If I trade with a Canadian, a Mexican, or an Englishman it is for the same reason that I trade with an American—that I would rather have the thing he gives me than the thing I give him. If I did not want the thing I am to get more than the thing I am to give, I would not wish to make the trade.[15]

This combined with other free trade arguments like the "free breakfast table", the idea that the most basic of goods would be more affordable without tariffs, convinced Cook that the implementation of free trade would be of benefit to working people. Cook's attitude to the "fiscal issue" is sometimes used as a prime example of his political inconsistency, as later as a leading member of the Commonwealth Liberal Party and the Nationalists he would begrudgingly accept keeping Australia's existing protectionist system. However, Ellis, who would have known Cook well, is clear that he remained "privately a Free Trader" for the rest of his life.[16] Thus Cook merely responded to circumstances where the political scene had clearly moved on from the debate, rather than actively abandoning his conviction.

In the same year as George's visit, Australia experienced the Great Maritime Strike which, along with the Shearers' Strike, would lead to the coming of the Labor Party. The former, which began as a conflict between the Steamship Owners' Association and the Mercantile Marine Officers' Association over an attempt to affiliate with the Melbourne Trades Hall, produced sympathy strikes including by coal miners whose output was then the essential fuel for much of the maritime industry.

Cook had considerable reservations about these sympathy strikes and did what he could to keep the Lithgow miners working. He had developed a reasonably cordial relationship with the local mine owners, and when he was compelled by the Labour Defence Committee to take up the strike (Lithgow being the last coal mining district to do so, after both Newcastle and the Illawarra), he openly expressed that it was a step "taken with sincere regret".[17] When the mine owners began bringing in non-union strike-breakers, Cook went to Sydney to try to lobby the Committee to let his miners return to work, and eventually they acquiesced. Later, when the Parkes Government set up a Royal Commission on Strikes, Cook would give evidence that he did not believe in the abrupt cessation of work in connection with labour disputes and advocated the setting up of boards of conciliation to settle conflicts as peacefully and amicably as possible. Citing an earlier example of a local strike he had resolved through "quiet talk" and "compromise", he claimed that he "never saw a dispute" which could not be settled in the same manner.[18]

The strikes would ultimately end in failure, putting tens of thousands out of work for months without securing any significant concessions. What was worse was that it occurred at the beginning of the 1890s depression, needlessly exacerbating the hardships that were to come. It was this failure which inspired the creation of the Labour Electoral Leagues, which sought to implement reform through Parliament now that the strike mechanism had proven futile.

As a leading unionist and figurehead for his region, Cook was naturally identified as a potential Labor candidate for the local seat of Hartley. However, he was initially hesitant fearing that he would lose his £40 deposit and not be able to pay scrutineers.[19] Cook was eventually persuaded to put his hand up by a number of supporters, including J. Ryan editor of the *Lithgow Mercury*. The local Labor organisation itself was tentative – though Hartley returned two members, they resolved to only run one candidate so as not to divide their efforts. Cook narrowly came second in the preselection, securing 395 votes while Reverend G.W. Smailes secured 398. However, the latter would ultimately have to withdraw due to influenza and the candidature fell to Cook.[20]

Cook's first election campaign was extremely short, there being less than two weeks between his accepting the Labor endorsement and the actual poll. Those that proposed his name at the public nomination of candidates emphasised the need for "direct representation of workers", though his support was broader than labour alone, for a Free Trade candidate by the name of J.P.T Caulfield withdrew his candidature to support Cook.[21] Cook's appeal to the voters emphasised the need to invest in education, introduce a comprehensive system of local government based on a land tax on unimproved values, and the need for federation to impose "absolute freedom of commercial intercourse between the colonies".[22] With the exception of opposing the 'imperialistic tendencies' of the federation model that had emerged from the 1891 Constitutional Convention (likely referring to the role of the Governor General and the maintenance of legal appeals to the Privy Council), none of this appeal was particularly radical and it could just as easily have been made by an ordinary Free Trade candidate. Indeed, the *Daily Telegraph* noted that Cook "is essentially a moderate man and more likely to go in for steady progressive legislation than for any policy of violent 'reconstruction of society'".[23] The progressive legislation Cook advocated included new coal mines regulations, the institution of the 8-hour day, the abolition of plural voting, and, notably, female suffrage (the latter perhaps a reflection of Cook's high regard for Mary's opinion on important matters).

At this time, elections were held over multiple days, and by the time of the Hartley poll it was already clear that the Labor candidates had won a large number of seats in

Sydney and were doing far better than anyone initially expected. This sense of momentum combined with Cook attracting the votes of regular Free Trade supporters saw him easily elected with 1028 votes.[24] Coming in second was the Free Trade candidate George Donald with 685. The two men got along very well and would frequently appear on the same platform together in the coming term, sharing a sense of responsibility for the district. Newspaper reactions to the result were generally positive, with the *Evening News* describing Cook as “a well read, highly intelligent, and unassuming man”, who being “more of a thinker than a talker…is not likely to trouble the Assembly with unnecessary speeches”.[25]

The Pledge

Labor’s emergence at the 1891 New South Wales election was a watershed moment in Australian political history. Out of nowhere, the new party won 35 seats in a Legislative Assembly of 141 and they immediately held the balance of power between the incumbent Free Trade Government and the Protectionist Opposition (though Labor itself was quite evenly split along fiscal lines). The men entering Parliament for the first time were political amateurs. Most were under forty and many were still in their twenties. Along with several miners like Cook there were ‘three or four printers, a boilermaker, three sailors, a plasterer, a journalist, a draper, a suburban mayor, two engineers, a carrier, a few shearers, a tailor, and—with bated breath—a mineowner, a squatter and an M.D.'[26]

They soon held their first caucus meeting where they determined not to elect a leader, and instead to rule by committee until they became more experienced at parliamentary methods. In line with union concepts of solidarity and obeying the decisions of branch meetings, they also adopted a pledge to "vote in the House as a majority of the party, sitting in caucus, has decided".[27] Party discipline was a novel and controversial innovation in NSW politics. The liberal tradition that had long held sway maintained that members needed to be able to vote as their conscience compelled them, and that to bind oneself to an outside force was an utter betrayal of both the electorate an individual represented and of the principles of representative government more broadly. The emergence of the fiscal parties had done little to alter this orthodoxy, as Henry Parkes had been temporarily put out of office in 1889 when eight nominal Free Traders had crossed the floor to vote against him.

Cook initially signed the pledge, but eight other Labor MPs refused to do so because they felt it might interfere with promises they had made during the election to support tariff protection. A compromise was offered in the form of a fiscal truce, in which caucus agreed that there should not be any change in tariff policy until the issue was decided by the people at a referendum. There was a great deal of naivety in this proposal, as indeed there was in the decision to delay electing a leader, and this would be proven immediately as Parliament met and a number of members defied caucus to vote for a censure motion moved by Protectionist Leader George Dibbs.

The Parkes Government survived the censure, but it would soon be brought down in a dispute over a new Coal Mines Regulation Bill in which Cook would unsurprisingly take an active part. The Bill initially mandated 8-hour days for workers aged between 14 and 17 but Cook successfully moved an amendment instituting a general 8-hour day in line with a policy he had been advocating since 1887. Cook also proposed increasing the ventilation prescribed for each miner from 100 cubic feet of pure air per minute to 150, and this was adopted in a vote of 29 to 10 while most of the members were out of the House.

This enlargement of the Bill's remit was, among other things, sure to make the process of getting it through the conservative Legislative Council extremely difficult. When the Bill was ready for its third reading that should have been largely a formality, influential Free Trade backbencher William McMillan moved that it should be recommitted.[28] He singled out the 8-hour provision, which he attacked as "unprecedented class legislation", as his motivation, and despite the fact that this was a government bill, Parkes decided to support the move. There followed some heated scenes in debate before the government was defeated on an adjournment motion that it decided to treat as a matter of confidence. This revealed another flaw in the Labor method, as there was no time for a caucus meeting to decide how to vote, and once again the party split, with Cook being one of just four Labor MPs who supported the Ministry. Cook was acting on a promise from the relevant Minister Sydney Smith that he would proceed with the Bill in two days' time, but Cook was also of the pragmatic view that getting new coal mines regulations passed was more important than getting everything he wanted included in one bill.

In the aftermath Parkes resigned as premier, Dibbs was commissioned to form a new government, and the outsider George Reid was elected as the Free Trade Party Leader.[29] Reid's attachment to free trade and to reform more generally was far deeper than that of Parkes, who was an old parliamentary manager who had essentially capitalised on the fiscal issue to regain office before largely abandoning it to pursue federation and the prestige that came with it. Reid on the other hand stood out as a conviction politician, who before the coming of the fiscal issue had been closely associated with the men who ended up forming the Protectionist Party, casting aside friendships in the name of principle. He was a charismatic and persuasive classical liberal, and in time he would earn Cook's deep admiration and help to liberalise his world-view.

When the new government rapidly proceeded to introduce

new tariffs under the justification that the depression had severely reduced revenue, Reid responded with a censure motion tailor-made to woo the Labor members. This attacked the government for distracting from a number of pieces of urgent reforming legislation by raising the fiscal issue, when the right thing to do was to carry on reforms such as an amendment to the *Electoral Act* to abolish plural voting (which allowed people to vote in multiple electorates if they owned multiple properties). Only in a new Parliament elected on 'one man, one vote' could the tariff issue be settled, or so Reid claimed.

This censure occasioned yet another Labor split, with the party dividing almost evenly into 17 for the motion and 16 against. Only one Labor member, the Protectionist James McGowen, voted against his fiscal interest. Half a party was enough Labor support for the Dibbs Government to survive, as it would for the remainder of the parliamentary term despite further censure attempts.

Over this period, Cook would emerge as a forceful parliamentary performer. He advocated for retrenchment in budgetary expenditure, particularly as an alternative to raising the tariff which he claimed took money out of the pockets of the people. He opposed the floating of loans in London and the accumulation of government debt, urging the state to live within its means. He also fought for the abolition of plural voting, taking aim at William Epps who had defended the practice for encouraging 'thrift'.

Cook was very thriftful, as his upbringing had forced him to be, but he pointed out that thrift was about more than acquiring property:

> A poor man with a large family earns £2 10s. a week. His ambition is to educate his children well, feed and clothe them decently, and at the end of 40 years he has no money. Epps' party do not consider that man thrifty, and would not give him an extra vote; but if that man had a £10 block of land and denied himself of some of the comforts of life to get it, he would be a thrifty man and get an extra vote. According to [Cook's] way of thinking the man who had lived respectably and properly educated and looked after his children would be the one to get the extra vote.[30]

At Bathurst in 1892, Cook gave an impassioned speech on the value of self-improvement. Repelled at the number of drunk MPs he had encountered in his short stint in Parliament (this was quite common in an era when the Assembly generally sat in the evening after members had tackled their ordinary jobs during the day), he declared that economic progress needed to be matched by moral progress if society were truly to improve:

> Men should use their spare moments in improving and cultivating their minds, and not in frivolity and other ways, which generally amounts to finding out the odds on certain horses, or requiring a nobbler in the morning, both of which practices unfitted them for the sterner duties of life... He would advise them not to neglect the quiet side of their lives, and they

> should try to get a grasp of all branches of learning. If men neglected to cultivate themselves the better men on the other side would eagerly take advantage, and would push them further back when an attempt was made to go forward. (Applause.) Let them improve themselves, and they would not only secure comfort and satisfaction for themselves, but make it a happier and brighter world for everyone.[31]

Cook would soon face his own moral test, as in the lead up to the next election Labor's extra-parliamentary organisation determined to solve the problem of disunity by imposing strict discipline on MPs. The first step taken was quite positive, for the organisation encouraged the parliamentary party to finally elect a leader and so Cook was subsequently unanimously voted in as the first Labor Parliamentary Leader in New South Wales. The choice reflected Cook's talents and the dedication which had seen him memorise parliamentary procedure with a level of detail his colleagues could not match. However, it also reflected the free trade majority within the party which meant the likewise talented McGowen was never really considered.

The second step was to institute a new and enlarged pledge, which after some debate was refined to the following:

> (a) A Parliamentary Labour Party, to be of any weight, must give a solid vote in the House upon all questions affecting the Labour Platform, the

> fate of the Ministry, or calculated to establish a monopoly, or to confer further privilege on the already privileged classes, as they arise; and,
>
> (b) that accordingly every candidate who runs in the Labour interest should be required to pledge himself, not only to the Fighting Platform and the Labour Platform, but also to vote on every occasion specified in Clause (a) as the majority of the Parliamentary Labour Party may in caucus decide.[32]

Cook was angered that the organisation seemed to view the current crop of parliamentary members as a group of failures, and he thought that this rigidity was precisely the problem which had caused so much division in the first place. He tried for months to lobby for a watering down of the pledge, but when this failed he issued a manifesto explaining why he and most of the parliamentary party could not submit to it. This claimed that the pledge was absurd, impractical and had clearly been written by people who had no experience of parliament for they failed to see that literally any vote could affect the fate of the ministry (as a simple adjournment motion had shown), and that it was impossible to hold a caucus meeting before every single vote. His manifesto also dismissed the pledge on more philosophic grounds:

> Perhaps the gravest objection to this pledge is the fact that it utterly destroys the representative character of the member. It is entirely undemocratic. It is a complete abrogation of the electoral privileges of the constituencies and seeks to vitiate

> the relationship which must always exist between the member and the electors. It absolutely prevents the making of any stipulations or compacts, which are the undoubted rights of the electors to demand before recording their votes. It seals the mouth of the candidate who has taken it. Outside the Labor platform he cannot, if he be honest, promise the electors, or any section of them, either to support or oppose any measure which they may desire to gain or reject. The result will be the alienation of such a large body of voters as will preclude the possibility of the candidate's return. The effect of this pledge has already been to drive from the leagues some of the staunchest members of the party, now called traitors, because they refuse to be slaves, it furnishes a ready weapon in the hands of those who openly declare that faithful service furnishes no claim for re-election, such declarations mean that, there shall be no reward for fidelity, intelligence, courage, and perseverance; and, on the other hand, no punishment for treachery, stupidity, cowardice, and inertia. It will be signed readily by candidates whose sole object is to get into Parliament by means of the Labor vote, but very reluctantly by the man who hesitates to promise something which might prove beyond his powers to perform.[33]

The introduction of the pledge set up one of the fundamental and enduring lines of cleavage in Australian politics, and Cook's attitude towards it immediately placed him in the liberal camp. Judith Brett has argued that it was the pledge, rather than any policy position, which ultimately separated social liberals like Alfred Deakin from the

Labor Party, despite them agreeing on many matters of state intervention, and it therefore defined Australia's party system.[34] Brett also links the pledge to a Protestant belief in the need to maintain moral independence and not submit to outside forces like the papacy, and while Cook was no sectarian his Methodism undoubtedly played a role in informing his position.[35]

Cook's entire life had been dedicated to forging a material and moral independence for himself, whereby through hard work and perseverance he had been able rise above the station of his birth and make decisions for himself as a man. While he was happy to voluntarily cooperate with others, did great community work in trying to alleviate the depression, and was a strong believer in what the unified action of the union movement had and could achieve, to ask him to permanently subordinate himself to group decision making was fundamentally against his character. His manifesto resolved that he would "refuse to be a slave", and it was this decision and the way it came to crystallise in his mind over the years which shaped his self-definition and would lead to a shift in outlook whereby his speeches and worldview increasingly emphasised individualism and freedom in a classically liberal manner. This was not merely the product of spending more time around liberal and conservative thinkers, in the manner in which it has generally been portrayed: it was about Cook and his agency.

The Reidite

The Hartley branch of the Labour Electoral League stood by Cook, convinced that he was defending their interests over the conspiracy of a city clique, and they were consequently declared "bogus" by the central administration. This was an emotional blow considering all the time and energy Cook had invested in the labour movement, but he was convinced that he would be proven correct when pledged members were unable to make dependable promises to their electorates and were consequently defeated at the polls.

The test would come soon enough with the 1894 election, held on a single day in July as a product of electoral reforms which had also abolished multi-member districts. Cook would contest the reduced Hartley electorate, having to compete with his friend George Donald, a pledged Labor candidate named John Henry and two others. His election speeches attacked extravagance in government spending, and called for the implementation of a land tax, mining on private lands, the suspension of crown land sales, and local option prohibition without compensation for license holders. In the end he easily topped the poll, with the particularly gratifying result being that Henry obtained a measly 17 votes compared to Cook's 723.[36] His supporters celebrated by carrying him aloft and marching through Lithgow with an accompanying band.[37]

Over NSW as a whole, Cook's prediction of the failure of

pledged men proved untrue, as 15 were elected compared to 8 'independent Labor' MPs. George Reid's Free Traders picked up a number of seats from a campaign which linked free trade to the introduction of direct land and income taxes which, combined with proposed economies in expenditure, would shift the financial burden of a restrained approach to government from ordinary people who paid the bulk of tariffs and on to the well off. This put Reid in the box-seat to form government with 61 Free Trade Members in an Assembly which was now composed of 124 seats (notwithstanding a strange ploy by Henry Parkes who wanted to be commissioned as premier despite not being the Free Trade Leader). However, 11 of these MPs were 'independent' Free Traders, so Reid would need the backing of at least the independent Labor men if he was to have any security.

Reid's reforming program naturally attracted them, and even the pledged Labor men would be fairly solid in supporting Reid for the next few years, but to make things a bit more certain Reid decided to offer Cook the ministerial position of Postmaster-General as a symbolic olive branch to working interests. Before this offer had been made, Cook had already stated publicly that he was excited about the election result providing a clear mandate for Reid to bring in a land tax.[38] Cook also said that while he was a supporter of federation, he thought the more pressing need was 'local government and a vigorous policy of decentralisation', an endorsement of Reid's plan to put federation on the backburner to focus on domestic reform. Reid for his part said in an interview that Cook had consistently given support to the Free Traders during the last Parliament, and that he had "shown on many occasions considerable powers of thought and debate without extravagance of views".[39]

Cook accepted the position after consulting his supporters. He in no way saw the decision as "selling out" his working-class roots. It was a natural progression for a man whose demonstrated talents had seen him elected Labor Leader, and he very much felt that he could have more influence within the Cabinet than outside of it. Reid's biographer notes that "the secret pride of working men in seeing one of their number in an important ministerial office was a real source of strength" for the Ministry, while in Cabinet Cook was an effective counterweight to some of the more conservative members.[40]

The opinion of Hartley would be gauged accurately and promptly, for NSW Parliament then still required ministers to face a by-election before attaining office. Despite their drastic failure at the recent poll, the Labor Central Executive spitefully decided to run a pledged candidate to try to oust Cook, and to add insult to injury they left most of the other ministers unopposed. A number of leading Labor figures visited Hartley to pour scorn on Cook during the campaign but Cook received his own support in the form of Ministers Jacob Garrard (who like him was a teetotal former trade unionist) and Sydney Smith. Cook was defiant, telling a meeting at Blackheath that he would "never sign away his individuality or his conscience for any caucus in the world", and the result was predictable, with Cook winning 942 to 182 (the extra "pledged" votes mainly coming from Protectionist supporters who did not have their own candidate).[41]

The position of Postmaster-General involved not just running the post office, but also responsibility for a range of telecommunications. At just 33 years of age Cook was comparatively young to be a minister, and he brought to the role his characteristic energy and dedication. Cook's primary task was cutting expenditure, as, though the Reid Government was determined to shift taxation to the well off, there was still a profound understanding that taxpayer money was literally taken from the people and spending must therefore be minimised. Cook was successful in his task, as "no opportunity for frugality was too small for him to overlook".[42] One of his more controversial cost-saving measures was to hire female telephonists who could be paid significantly less than men.

It was not all penny pinching though – the responsibility for telephones and telegraphs meant that Cook could also spearhead notable innovations. An avid reader as always, he kept up to date with the latest developments in Europe and North America. Cook helped to expand the NSW telephone network such that it became larger, in terms of lines, than all the other Australian Colonies combined – a feat helped by the fact that Cook introduced the first long distance phoneline between Sydney and Newcastle.[43] He standardised regulations, cut telephone fees to encourage adoption, introduced coin-slot public payphones, pushed for underground telephone lines for reasons of safety and aesthetics, and also led the wave of adopting the bicycle as a swift method of letter delivery.

Cook's wowser views were reflected in the fact that he cracked down on people using letters to conduct betting and took responsibility for a Local Option Bill that was outside of his ministerial purview (this was essentially a private member's bill that allowed the government to placate a widespread prohibitionist movement, even though Reid did not agree with the cause). Despite this belief in moral restriction and often being described as humourless, Cook had a warm sense of humour that comes across frequently on the pages of Hansard. Time spent around the jovial Reid served to further lighten him up. He did not take up the demon drink, but he did adopt the habit of smoking cigars and bought a piano and a portable organ for his new two-storey home in the centre of Lithgow.

Despite their somewhat contrasting personalities, Cook and Reid had a natural affinity for each other. Biographer John Murdoch has argued that Cook had a psychological need to seek out father figures, and through his loyal subordination to Reid, Deakin and Billy Hughes they all ultimately filled that role for him.[44] His relationship with Reid was not comparable to the other two, however. He accepted far more of Reid's world view, whereas he was compromising with former adversaries when dealing with the others. The two men became lifelong friends, to the extent that Cook visited Reid on his deathbed in England in 1918, though tragically Reid had already slipped out of consciousness by the time his old deputy arrived.[45] Cook's sentimental comments on Reid's passing do back up the father-figure relationship, as Cook said that "I always regarded it a privilege and a delight to give him my best" – giving a sense that he had a strong desire to make his leader proud.[46] Reid for his part appreciated Cook's dedication and had his own admiration for Cook's astounding rise from Staffordshire, remarking in his memoirs "how many millions of chances to one there must have been against such a destiny", and on other occasions holding Cook up as an example for school children to emulate.[47]

Reid would earn Cook's respect in the early years through his decisive method of government. He did not back-down when the un-elected Legislative Council inevitably tried to block his direct taxation measures. Instead, he called a snap election in 1895 (at which pledged Labor wisely chose not to contest Hartley) and produced a result which forced the Council to acquiesce. In his first Parliament Cook had been dismayed at the inertia and difficulty of getting legislation through. Though Reid did not get everything he wanted, notably his Local Government Bill had to be abandoned, it was a period of accomplishment then unequalled in NSW political history, and thus a stark contrast to that first experience. Land and income taxes were passed, trade was made truly free to a far greater extent than it had been under Parkes let alone Dibbs, NSW led the way in economic recovery, important land reforms were undertaken, the public service was reformed to make it efficient and abolish patronage, there was also a new Coal Mines Regulation Bill, and a new Factories and Shops Bill.[48]

No-Yes Cook

The federation issue had lain somewhat dormant since the surprise result of the 1891 election, but in late 1895, having made solid progress on his domestic agenda, Reid decided to breathe new life into the project by picking up a suggestion for a new series of Constitutional Conventions made up of elected delegates. Cook's attitude towards the issue was like many New South Welshmen, in that he supported the idea in principle but was concerned about the details, both in terms of how many sacrifices his Colony would have to make and how much bending of the hard-won "one man, one vote" ideal a federal compact would involve. Unlike many Labor men, Cook was also a believer in subsidiarity, the idea that political decisions should be made at the most local level that is practicable in order to achieve the best outcomes, and he therefore had a distaste for unnecessary centralisation (which undoubtedly would have been reinforced by his dealings with both union and Labor central executives).

Cook did not seek election as a delegate for the Conventions, as the Reid Government decided to run only three candidates for ten available positions so as not to unnecessarily politicise the process. During the first referendum campaign Cook took his time before making a public utterance, but he eventually gave a speech at Lithgow explaining why he was voting "no".[49] He criticised the Senate for being undemocratic, not only for giving equal representation to each State regardless of population but also for being voted in as a State-wide electorate which was too large for the "demos" to have influence. He pointed to Germany and Canada as examples of federations that did not give equal representation to each constituent part, complaining that delegates had "slavishly copied the American type". He was also opposed to the "Braddon Blot" which seemed to necessitate tariffs by keeping State governments reliant on their revenue, and he suggested that centralising the post office and other departments was no guarantee of increased efficiency.

Hartley supported Cook's position, producing a comfortable "no" majority though like many electorates the turnout was low.[50] Overall, Sydney voted "no" and the referendum failed to reach the minimum number of "yes" votes (though "yes" did have a majority thanks to the strength of its vote in the country districts).[51] In the aftermath, it was clear that the Constitution would have to be slightly altered to placate NSW and the Colony went to an election to essentially determine whether Reid or Edmund Barton (who headed what had been the Protectionists) would lead the negotiations. For his views on the referendum, Cook was opposed in Hartley by the ardent-federalist J.F. Tabrett, but he easily saw him off receiving more than 70 per cent of the vote. Notably, during the election campaign Cook would defend the government as "champions of liberalism", and while the Free Traders had restyled themselves as the "Liberal Federal Party" as opposed to Barton's "National Federal Party", this marked one of the first instances in which Cook would publicly conceptualise himself as a liberal.[52]

The election saw the Reid Government returned with a reduced majority, and the NSW Premier would secure a number of constitutional concessions including more democratic provisions for resolving a deadlock between the two Houses, a limit on the term of the Braddon clause, and that the capital site would be within NSW but at least 100 miles from Sydney. This was enough to convince Cook to support "yes" at the second referendum, conducting an extensive speaking tour of NSW's mining districts in support of the cause, though there were also practical party reasons for changing his position. The *Daily Telegraph* was prompt to point out his inconsistency, reprinting Cook's old speeches as part of the 'in the witness box' series it used to campaign for a "no" vote.[53] The "no" case was still strongly supported by the pledged Labor men, but their efforts were to no avail as the second referendum succeeded in making federation a done deal.

While Cook's role in the politics of federation was somewhat limited, Kevin Livingstone has demonstrated that as Postmaster-General Cook played an important role in promoting "technological federation".[54] This included chairing two intercolonial post and telegraph conferences aimed at improving communication channels between the Colonies in a manner that would play a vital role in facilitating the practicalities and shared culture of the new nation.

Among the seats the government lost at the election were those of three ministers, and this necessitated a Cabinet reshuffle which saw Cook become Minister for Mines and Agriculture. This was obviously a dream posting, and the likely reason it had not been offered to Cook in 1894 was because at the time this would have been seen as too radical.

Cook was able to rectify an old bugbear from his time as a checkweighman by signing an executive order ensuring that every skip of coal was weighed in the calculation of miners' pay, rather than averaging from limited samples. Holding the post for just over a year, he also put considerable work into formulating new coal mines regulations and a scheme of compulsory unemployment insurance, and while this legislation was not passed before the Reid Government fell, much of it would be picked up by the incoming government (which relied on Labor support and therefore had a vested interest in pursuing these issues). On the agricultural front, Cook drove innovation by employing a government wheat experimentalist, increased quarantine protocols, ensured that farmers were instructed on the latest methods of disease control, and instituted a Colony-wide butter competition in the name of raising standards for export. Recognition of his achievements was given by the governments of Queensland and New Zealand, who for the first time in a generation allowed the import of NSW fruit.[55]

The Reid Government was brought down in September 1899 by a combination of a small number of disaffected Free Traders and the Labor Party, which switched its support to the Opposition after it dumped Barton for William Lyne. Labor's decision was allegedly manipulated by the "solid six", a group of MPs including Billy Hughes who threated to resign from the Labor Party if caucus did not vote their way.[56] The ensuing censure debate was a classic example of men being compelled to vote against their conscience, with McGowen practically giving a 'eulogy' of all the things he liked about the Reid Government before proceeding to vote it out of office.[57] There is little doubt that the experience can only have hardened Cook's distaste for the pledge and the men who submitted to it.

Relieved of ministerial duties, Cook made good use of his free time raising money for a local hospital and serving as secretary of the Poor Relief Society. His increasingly imperialistic views were reflected in his support for the Boer War and letters to newspapers advocating for the full retention of Privy Council appeals post-federation. But while some things changed, others stayed the same, for Cook continued to lobby for the 8-hour day, spoke out in favour of female suffrage on the grounds that a woman's judgement was just as sound as a man's, and had success with a private member's Truck Bill banning wages being paid in kind rather than in money (another issue he had encountered in his Staffordshire days).[58]

Soon enough, all eyes turned towards the inauguration of the Commonwealth on 1 January 1901, and Cook had to ponder whether he would stand for the new Federal Parliament. Cook was initially inclined to stick with State politics and potentially become Leader of the Opposition, which had the advantage of not requiring frequent trips to the "temporary" capital in Melbourne for only a fractionally higher salary and no travel allowance. However, he was eventually induced to run for Parramatta as his personal popularity would greatly assist the Free Traders to win the seat, hence the decision was yet another act of loyalty towards Reid.

Cook based his election pitch on representing the interests of New South Wales as part of a "good fighting phalanx" of

Free Traders who would stand up for the fiscal system that had made their State rich and prosperous.[59] He attacked Parramatta's Protectionist candidate William Sandford (proprietor of an iron and steel mill) as a representative of the manufacturing class, who wanted to take money from the people to help his sectional interests.[60] Cook rejected the idea that tariff barriers were needed to foster local industries, suggesting that the only healthy and efficient industries would be those that could succeed without artificial help. He also linked free trade to a broader acceptance of freedom in a given society, pointing to the positive example of Switzerland "which led the whole world in genius, human liberty, and reason", while viewing Protectionist America as synonymous with big tycoons and corruption.[61]

Beyond the fiscal issue, Cook had quite a limited view of what the Federal Government should do, which fitted with his subsidiarity beliefs. He dismissed Barton's proposal for old age pensions by pointing out that the Braddon clause required 3/4ths of tariff revenue be returned to the States, and hence only the States would have the money for such a scheme until the "blot" could be removed. He was sceptical of federal legislation on conciliation and arbitration considering the Constitution would limit its jurisdiction, and he opposed the amalgamation of State railways because those of NSW were making a profit while others were more poorly run. On the question of defence, he supported a "citizen soldiery" over a standing army, while on the pervasive populist issue of White Australia he insisted that Queensland's Pacific Islander labourers be deported as swiftly as possible because they were being used to undercut fair wages.

It was enough to see Cook comfortably elected 5,778 to 3,646, overcoming what was considered to be a large investment of the Protectionists' resources in trying to win the seat.[62] Over the nation as a whole, the Protectionists benefitted from their somewhat perverse incumbency (a Barton Ministry having been sworn in before the elections were even held) to narrowly edge the Free Traders 31 seats to 28, while Labor secured 14 and the balance of power.[63] It was a heartening result for Reid's men nonetheless, and they celebrated with a lavish picnic at the picturesque Port Hacking Heads. There the soon-to-be Leader of the Federal Opposition heaped praise on Cook as "one of his most esteemed, worthy and able colleagues", promising that he would be in Reid's ministry when the time came to form one.[64]

The Member for Parramatta

When the full Free Trade Party met before the opening of Parliament, they duly elected Reid leader despite his warning that he would have significant absences to keep up his legal practice. Sir William McMillan was elected deputy, both on the grounds of seniority (he was Parkes' old Treasurer) and reconciliation (for he and fellow Free Trade MP Bruce Smith had become estranged from Reid and ran unsuccessfully as Barton candidates at the 1898 election).

Cook thus carried with him only limited status from his successes in the NSW Parliament. In his first speech he had a fiery exchange with Deakin over whether there was more poverty in Protectionist America or Free Trade Britain. Cook tried to make a name for himself by moving an amendment to the Address in Reply criticising the government for being vague on White Australia, but this was premature and attracted little support even amongst his own party.[65]

Despite this early setback, Cook was able to find his feet in the marathon debates over the first tariff. This was an exercise in sheer endurance in which he excelled, fighting item by item for a reduction in the level of taxation, particularly on basic goods, sometimes with success. Cook was always quick to interject, raise a point of order, and fully engage in the fight. He could sometimes go too far, as when he accused a Victorian MP of having "turned dog on the men who put you into Parliament", a remark which the Speaker made him withdraw.[66] A Melbourne reporter described his early impressions of Cook as being "pugnacious, though his pugnacity is accompanied by a good tempered face", while he was also listed as one of those who had perfected the art of 'scientific stonewalling'.[67]

Cook fought the fiscal battle both inside and outside of Parliament, holding large meetings in his electorate where he emphasised the way in which Barton's allegedly "moderate tariff" was greatly and inconsistently raising prices. Taxes on a gentlemen's silk hat had been raised 25 per cent but a poor man's felt hat had been raised 125 per cent; boots and other items had a similar discrepancy, which was deliberate and justified under the pretext of 'keeping the shoddy out'. As Cook pointed out, this was little consolation to the working man, who often could only afford such "shoddy" items and would now have to go without. "The tariff ranged anywhere from 25 to 150 per cent, and averaged at least 45 or 50 per cent" as "everything was piled on to the shoulders of the workers, while the rich were relieved".[68] On another occasion, Cook pointed to the impact of the tariff on poor families and suggested that "no man ought to be in the position of Minister for Trade and Customs unless he had at least ten children" – leaving himself one short of the benchmark.[69]

While Cook was thus a highly effective Oppositionist, he provided more constructive criticism on pet issues to do with the post office, undersea cables, and the interests of fruit growers. The latter was peculiarly specific to his seat, which even had a local newspaper called *The Cumberland Argus and Fruitgrowers' Advocate*. While he took care of his community, Cook proved that he was not a mere delegate and would stand up for principle by opposing bounties for the iron industry that were heavily favoured around

Lithgow but were an anathema to Cook's idea of ensuring healthy businesses could stand on their own two feet. Sandford, whose company was personally affected by this decision, organised mass rallies at which Cook was burned in effigy, but he did not back down in the face of such intimidation.[70]

Perhaps Cook's most interesting contribution during the Commonwealth's first term was on the Defence Bill, where he critiqued conscription and compulsory training in favour of sponsoring rifle clubs and having a more organic citizens' militia. He spoke out against the widespread introduction of military disciple into society as something that could destroy what was great about the Australian character. Responding to Billy Hughes, Cook said:

> He seems to regard the proposal as one for the physical development and discipline of our growing population by means of athletic exercises and hopes thereby to get rid of certain qualities in the young Australians which, he says, are deplorable, but which I do not think are of as great moment as he imagines. I am aware that there is a certain amount of larrikinism in Australia... those characteristics which people deplore are the result of the natural rebound from the dull grey industrial Gradgrind existence of older countries. It is because of the greater freedom and the better conditions under which we live, that our young people show more blithesomeness and gaiety and animal spirits. Of course, a certain amount of discipline is required to

> impart steadiness to our national character, but I should be very sorry to see all those qualities which tend to make life happy and free, and glad, and spontaneous, disciplined out of existence.[71]

This was a remarkable display of Cook's specific patriotism, one which despite his growing attachment to the Crown and Empire, had special affection for what was distinct and joyous about his adoptive home. It shows that Cook was nowhere near as uptight as his teetotalism and devout religion might have you believe, but it also gives an insight into his gradual shift towards what opponents dubbed 'conservatism'. With his tremendous sense of perspective, Cook understood that things were comparatively very good under Australia's existing liberal order, and he became determined to preserve key elements of it. The *Sunday Times* was quite captivated by Cook's speech, using it as the basis for a couple of humour pieces with titles like "The Ballad of Blithesome Bill".[72]

Cook had always prided himself on having one of the highest parliamentary attendance records and this carried over into federal politics. At the end of the first term, he had been present for 254 of 298 sitting days, which ranked fourth of all the New South Welshman.[73] The Free Traders' cause was quite inhibited by the fact that two of the worst attendance records belonged to Reid and the retiring McMillan. To make matters worse, the government had thrown out the results of a review into electoral boundaries which was contrary to its self-interest, preserving an effective gerrymander which greatly favoured the NSW Protectionists' rural seats and which was exacerbated by the introduction of female voters who were more concentrated in urban areas. A fierce believer in equally weighting votes, Cook was aghast at the sight of "politicians 'fiddling' while the charter of liberty is burned" and was frequently reprimanded for his open use of the "g" word in the House.[74]

The one silver lining was that a proposal to redistribute Lithgow out of Parramatta was obstructed, so Cook was able to prove that his supporters had not abandoned him over the iron bonus, even though he had by now moved to Marrickville to be closer to the Melbourne trainline. Sandford declined to test him, and the Protectionists had to belatedly scrounge for a candidate in an effort which several newspapers suggested was purely intended to keep Cook from having too much spare time to speak in support of other Free Traders.[75] In the end he did venture outside his electorate, taking the opportunity to shoot down Sandford's chances at obtaining Macquarie over Sydney Smith, while still managing to garner over 80 per cent of the vote for Parramatta.[76]

Nation-wide the result was what Deakin would famously dub the "three elevens", meaning that there was one too many teams for a functioning game of cricket, as Labor gains resulted in three near-evenly represented parties in the House of Representatives and what would prove to be a period of incredible political instability. Cook once again missed out on the deputy leadership of the Free Trade Party, but this time he was at least considered a significant contender. He was the preferred choice of the "radical members", but the more conservative Dugald Thomson got the nod.[77]

The Protectionist Government continued, now with Deakin as Prime Minister, until it was defeated on a Labor-sponsored amendment to the Conciliation and Arbitration Bill which tried to include State instrumentalities in its provisions. There was much debate as to whether including the States was constitutional, and Reid decided not to vote for the amendment because of this, but Cook was happy to let the matter be judged by the High Court and eager to see the government go down. The debate was protracted and the result predictable, such that when on a separate matter the Labor Member for Kalgoorlie asked Deakin to launch an inquiry into Italian immigration to Western Australia, Cook jokingly asked "Cannot the honourable member wait, and make the inquiry himself?".[78]

After Deakin's resignation there was genuine speculation that Cook might be asked to join the new Labor Government to give it added ballast, with the *Sydney Morning Herald* suggesting that he remained nearly as radical as the pledged party.[79] In the end he did not join the Watson Ministry, but nor would Cook be there to oppose it for he was soon struck down with a severe bout of what was variously labelled rheumatism or neuritis and which kept him house bound for almost two months. Some speculated that the incessant train trips were to blame for the ailment which took such a hold of Cook's back and shoulder that even when he did return, he remained so blistered and sore that wearing a winter overcoat was an ordeal.

While Reid did visit Cook while he was housebound, Cook's illness meant that he was cut off from at least the early stages of lengthy negotiations which sought to create a coalition out of the Free Traders and the less radical Protectionists – a proposition he was later revealed to have serious misgivings about. One of the issues the two groups agreed on was opposing Labor additions to the Conciliation and Arbitration Bill including giving the Court the power to preference unionists in employment. This was a breach of equality before the law and touched on a long-standing liberal opposition to enshrined privilege which went all the way back to debates surrounding the attempt to establish a "Bunyip aristocracy". One of the defining features of the free country Cook had lauded when debating the Defence Bill was that there was no established church or peerage, and that individuals had been afforded a level playing field on which they could compete and succeed. Combined with prosperity driven by relatively low taxes, this had facilitated a huge degree of social mobility and engrained egalitarianism into the national character.

Cook was not yet opposed to all forms of union preference, but he did object to Labor's proposal as being "contrary to the spirit and purpose of a genuine trade union".[80] This stance was irritating to Minister for External Affairs Billy Hughes, who sent a number of telegrams to Cook lobbying for his support on the Bill without success. In the acrimonious debate which preceded the fall of the Watson Government, Hughes let loose his frustration by launching into an unprovoked attack on Cook as a Labor traitor:

> From such a galaxy as is presented by honourable members opposite, one hesitates whom to select. Take the honourable member for Parramatta, who during the whole of this discussion has said nothing. There is wisdom, the wisdom of the serpent, of Satan himself; because whatever he had said would have exposed him to the inevitable consequences of his inconsistency... He can never rid himself of the fact that he proposes now to throw over those very people upon whose shoulders he has climbed up.[81]

Cook interjected that it was the Labor Party who had tried to rub him out for not signing the pledge, and that the workers of Lithgow continued to support him. Hughes then made another reference to Satan which earned the rebuke of the Speaker, before accusing Cook of having been bribed to leave the Labor Party by the Postmaster job. Cook pointed out that this was historically false, and claimed that he had never been in the same Labor Party as Hughes, because the original Labor Party had been declared 'bogus' by the Central Executive which then created the new pledged entity.

The exchange was vicious but in some respects cathartic. As much as Cook's views had evolved, the Labor Party itself was moving away from the limited reformist program of its early years and would soon adopt the infamous "socialist objective". In such circumstances, it would supplant the Protectionists as the greatest threat to the liberal order that had developed in NSW, and which Cook had increasingly grown to appreciate. Hughes' hatred and blasphemy helped to ensure that as Cook's liberalism compelled him to become a warrior for anti-socialism, he could make the transition with a clear conscience.

The Anti-Socialist Campaign

Reid's task of forming a coalition ministry was a careful and difficult balancing act, made all the more hazardous by Deakin's refusal to join (though he did promise support). Outside of the prime minister, there were only three spots for Free Traders and with Cook's recent health scare he was passed over. By all accounts he took the news graciously, which is more than can be said for the *Fruitgrowers' Advocate* which repeatedly complained that Cook could have been NSW Premier by now if it was not for Reid's intervention.[82] Cook was more concerned about the consequences of working with a number of Protectionists, and he embarrassed the government by declining a seat on

Reid's new Tariff Commission because he felt that body would give a platform to sectional demands.

The new government proposed to finally pass a Conciliation and Arbitration Bill which had already brought down two ministries. In the bigger picture, Reid sought to vanquish the three elevens which had served to undermine responsible government and disenfranchise the people (whose votes seemed to have less effect on who was to govern them than the machinations of politicians), by moving beyond the fiscal issue and uniting the forces of liberalism. Only in a two-party system, it seemed, could there be stable majorities where the electorate could directly choose the government.

Reid did not have to look far for inspiration, for in New South Wales his friend and former minister Joseph Carruthers had already succeeded in imposing clear "lines of cleavage" on politics, based around a philosophic divide over the role of the state.[83] On one side was Labor with its increasing socialism, and on the other a self-consciously centre-right form of liberalism, which remained committed to reform and was not laissez-faire. It nevertheless distinguished itself with a commitment to keeping taxation and spending within reasonable bounds and leaving the individual free to pursue their own ends. Other key dividing lines were sectionalism (for example, union preference) versus 'governing for all', and of course the pledge versus liberty of conscience. These issues were not limited to NSW, as Victoria had also experienced the small government 'Kyabram Movement' which responded to the significant increase in the size and burden of the state which accompanied federation. However, as a template for stabilising a Lower House, Carruthers' example was unmatched.

Reid had a strong cause around which to push for a realignment, for in Labor circles there had been a mounting campaign to adopt the "socialist objective" of nationalising the means of production, distribution and exchange. In early 1905, this would enter the Federal Labor Platform as the slightly milder "collective ownership of monopolies, and the extension of the industrial and economic functions of the state", giving a great spur to what would become George Reid's famous anti-socialist campaign.[84]

Cook had already enunciated his position on socialism in a discussion which led on from his exchange with Hughes. He said that while he would do his best to uplift "all who have to toil for their daily bread" he was opposed to socialism because "the element of private gain was the great industrial motive power". Cook did not wish to see individuals subsumed by the collective because:

'I believe that the socialistic system which has been preached from the hilltops would in the end lead to an intolerable tyranny with our present human nature, so that it would of itself break down... The sweep of natural laws is a fact to be reckoned with, and all your Parliaments cannot ultimately defeat and overthrow them. If we can work with them, if we can harness and guide them, so that they will move our way, we shall be following the path to industrial peace and permanent prosperity; but if we go in the teeth of them, and attempt to scotch them, we shall be courting disaster, disintegration, and decay.'[85]

This belief in natural law flowed from Cook's religious beliefs, but there is evidence that he had also been reading Edmund Burke and may therefore have been influenced by his views on the inherent wisdom hidden within how practices had evolved over multiple generations.[86] As Cook put the socialism question on another occasion, "it is one thing to see that labour gets its fair apportionment of the fruits of the industrial tree ... it is another thing to lay the axe at its root in a mad endeavour to bring it down".[87] Free enterprise and capitalism were the well-springs of prosperity, and Cook's solution to workers' equity was to encourage labour and capital to cooperate more and engage in things like profit sharing. In contrast, socialism seemed to thrive on class conflict and divisions which Cook had always seen as toxic even at the height of his union activity. He frequently quoted official statistics on housing and other standards of living to prove that most Australians were remarkably well off, wealth was widely spread, and that of all places to risk revolution this was not it.

Ever the political combatant, Cook seems to have relished

the advent of the anti-socialist campaign which gave him relief from the uneasy compromises of the coalition. He delivered speeches where he declared that a socialistic Commonwealth would result in “Common-want”, he debated Watson on the contradictions of Christian socialism, and he served as deputy chairman and chief recruiter for the Australian Liberal League, the new extra-parliamentary organisation the Anti-Socialists established with a view to fighting the upcoming election.[88]

The early stages of the anti-socialist campaign did little to solidify the coalition, for when Parliament resumed in late June 1905 Deakin withdrew his support and the government fell. In the heated debate which naturally accompanied proceedings, Cook indulged in giving his chief an “I told you so” about how he had warned Reid that Deakin could not be trusted and would inevitably wreck the coalition, and the outgoing prime minister had little choice but to reply with a melancholic “hear hear”.[89] Reid asked for a dissolution of the House, but this was refused by the Governor General who was assured by Deakin that he could form a government, this time explicitly relying on Labor support. Deakin had no mandate, and his desire to avoid letting the people have a say after three governments had already fallen was easy for opponents to construe in a negative light.

In the wash-up Cook would be rewarded for his foresight, for in July 1905 he was finally and unanimously elected deputy leader. This would prove to be a crucial role, as far from abandoning his campaign, Reid's loss of government spurred him to double down on an unprecedented national speaking tour in an effort to fundamentally reshape the political divide. This tour involved long periods away from the House, where Cook would function as the head of the Opposition. As the *Sydney Morning Herald* reported:

> There are few men in the House of wider knowledge, and fewer who are able debaters. Mr. Cook is a great fighter. He is well versed in all the points of party combat, and as a speaker has a bright but stirring and convincing style. Next to making good speeches perhaps a Parliamentarian's best service to his cause is to spoil those of members on the other side. As an interjector, Mr. Cook stands only behind Mr. Reid in the Federal Parliament. On dozens of occasions a well timed remark of his has ridiculed and wrecked the effect of ambitious orations that had been weeks under preparation.[90]

While it undoubtedly remained a handicap for the Opposition not to have its Leader in the House, Cook and Reid formed a highly effective partnership considering the circumstances. Cook kept the Deakin Government honest and under sustained attack, while Reid was free to focus on appealing directly to the people. With Deakin's reliance on the pledged caucus he had already denounced and pursuit of a legislative program tailored to appease it, there were plenty of issues that Cook could rhetorically exploit, and he managed to put up such an effective stonewall that the government was forced to introduce extraordinary gag measures to shut down debate. It was this period which would lead Reid to write in his memoirs, "the able and devoted services of Mr. Joseph Cook, as deputy leader of the opposition, were the main factors in making my position tolerable. Had he been less able, or less loyal, or less devoted than he was, a leadership so long and so often suspended as mine could not have lasted for a single session".[91]

Outside of the House, Cook continued to make a concerted contribution to the anti-socialist campaign, including conducting an expansive speaking tour of regional Victoria. In another significant time commitment, Cook produced an extended essay for *The Citizen* magazine, which endeavoured to prove that socialism was the "resurrection" of an old idea that had been tried and failed numerous times from Pericles onwards, and which marshalled quotations from St. Paul and several early church fathers to defend "the law of competition".[92] Cook would build on these theological themes with a speech he delivered at Hurstville, where he said:

> Rights were not derived from society, but were natural, and given by the Creator Himself. Individual rights involved individual obligations and duties, and in carrying them out virtue power, and personality were produced. Therefore, socialism, aiming at the development of a condition which sought to merge the individual in the mass,

> sought to deprive him of his obligations and responsibilities, and the motive for intelligence and personality were taken away, and the opportunities for their production ceased.

Here you can see how Cook's views on socialism were shaped by and enmeshed with his own personal story. Imposing equality of outcomes and homogenising humanity destroyed the impetus behind the philosophy of self-improvement which had been Cook's personal creed from his earliest days. Any society in which individuals were not held to account for their own actions, and instead just averaged out, would inevitably lead to first the erosion of morals and then to the retrogression of progress. With all the emphasis on Cook's alleged inconsistency of beliefs, people seem to have missed that his conclusions on this fundamental issue were inherent in his conception of self.

Deakin clung to office as long as constitutionally possible, finally calling an election for 12 December 1906. Despite having made himself a huge target, Cook was unopposed in Parramatta and free to lend his assistance to a whole host of candidates across NSW and even southern Queensland. He even took the time to write a letter to the editor of the *Sydney Morning Herald* disputing a claim that the up-and-coming British politician Winston Churchill was a socialist.[93]

In the end the anti-socialist campaign came remarkably close to achieving its goal. Reid's party received 47.4 per cent of the vote in the Senate, more than 10 percentage points higher than any single party had ever received and tantalisingly close to an outright majority.[94] In the House of Representatives things remained far more fractured. Federation had created an imagined community that had little practical cohesion, and while Reid's immense touring was an effort to overcome this, it was too much to be achieved in just one campaign. Deakin's party was left with a mere 16 seats, but the anti-socialist vote was split between the main party, a handful of independent Anti-Socialist Protectionists (including Robert Menzies' uncle Sydney Sampson), and two members of the short-lived "Western Australian Party". Once again, the choice of who was to govern would be left up to the machinations of politicians.

The Fusion

Deakin once again continued in office with Labor support and determined to introduce a fully protective tariff that would dwarf what had come before it. Labor still had a number of nominal free traders and had to be careful not to alienate its voters in New South Wales, but the party was by and large won over by the lure of so-called "new protection". This promised that protective tariffs would only be given to industries that paid high wages, and thus it would allegedly ensure that workers would benefit in a manner that offset the pain they would feel as consumers.

Cook was instinctively sceptical. He pointed out that there were constitutional limitations that would inhibit the implementation of the plan, that the high costs of the tariff would be paid by all regardless of whether they were privileged to work for a protected industry, that Australia's vital exporting primary industries would be disadvantaged, that there remained no proven link between protectionism and increased wages, and that the tariff would be passed first so the bargain could not be guaranteed.[95] Tariffs high enough to fully protect an industry would raise little revenue as few goods would be imported, so they would also necessitate new taxes. Cook had supported direct taxation in NSW when it was either that or tariffs, but to have both and to have direct taxes levied by both State and federal governments would hugely increase the burden felt by all levels of society and also negatively impact on prosperity. Cook suspected that this is why Labor supported new protection, that it was ultimately part of a plot to overthrow the existing economic system.

It was a depressing time to be a free trader, and Cook could have been forgiven for giving up. This is what Reid was accused of doing, with the *Daily Telegraph* suggesting that he "surrendered before a shot was fired, and went off to Sydney".[96] However, in typical Cook fashion he stayed and fought, item by item, hour by hour, long into many nights. The results were admirable and earned Cook widespread praise. He won reductions on wire netting and fodder to help drought affected farmers, rallying free trade morale, and leading to further successful amendments on paper, glass, linen, sheep vaccines, and many more. It could hardly be called a victory, but it was a dignified and mitigated defeat.

While the tariff passed, in June 1908 several of Cook's warnings about new protection were vindicated by the High Court, which decided that the taxation power could not be used by the Australian Parliament to indirectly regulate working conditions. This would help to precipitate the end of the Deakin-Labor alliance, for new Labor Leader Andrew Fisher wanted the Constitution amended to overcome the difficulty, but Deakin was hesitant on the details as full industrial powers would open the door for full socialism.[97] Cook delighted in fanning the flames of division, suggesting to the House that Labor had been "cheated" by the government and had succeeded only in helping to pass "old protection".[98]

By now there was a general sense that the moment for the long-awaited political realignment might finally have come. One of the sources of ongoing tension between the fiscal parties was relieved with the resolving of the capital site issue. This was a long battle of NSW vs Victoria in which Cook had naturally played a leading role, and the choice of Yass-Canberra was viewed as a significant victory for his side (and some consolation for the tariff).

Reid sent out an olive branch by making a public offer that

both he and Cook would be willing to vacate their positions if it might help provide a "fresh footing" for liberals to coalesce.[99] What Cook privately thought of this we do not know. He had been against the original coalition and unlike Reid he had been down in the trenches of the recent tariff fight, so it must have been hard to be conciliatory. Nevertheless, the socialism issue still loomed large in his mind, and he was keen to protect the Constitution through a healthy two-party system and a thorough defence of the principles of federalism. A Labor backlash at the High Court's decision loomed ominously – the Party had labelled it "partisan', displaying little respect for the necessary restraints that made parliamentary government work, and raised the possibility that Labor might stack the court.

The Labor Party finally withdrew its support for Deakin in November, Fisher formed a minority government, and negotiations for a "fusion" stepped up in pace.[100] Reid did indeed step aside, but Cook did not have to, and was elected the new leader of the Anti-Socialists with his predecessor's full backing. What Cook did have to do was make a large number of sacrifices to achieve the desired merger: Deakin would be head of the new party, the tariff would be kept and anomalies resolved on a protectionist basis, a fresh attempt to facilitate new protection was promised, and Cook would have to accept the compulsory military training scheme he had criticised as illiberal. This was a lot, but at least the tariff was not to be increased, and it was not likely to be overturned in the immediate future in any case. Not only had the issue largely exhausted itself domestically but the international climate had turned. When the Free Traders had first started getting behind federation, they were riding high off the 1892 presidential election of Grover Cleveland which seemed to indicate that the world was on the path towards a widespread liberalising of trade. But since then, there had been a rising tide of economic nationalism in the lead up to the First World War and even in Britain the Gladstonian system was under fierce attack from people like Joseph Chamberlain.

Looking past the protection issue, Cook and his following could afford to play the long game, confident that their more classical understanding of liberalism would win out against the state-expanding "social liberalism". Not only did they have a numerical advantage in the new party stemming from the 1906 election result, but Deakin's most radical followers refused to join at all. In this sense, the future looked bright.

After more than half a year of negotiations, the "Deakin-Cook" Ministry was sworn in on 2 June 1909.[101] Cook took the position of Minister for Defence, for at the time security concerns were a high national priority. Germany was in the middle of a naval arms race with Great Britain and active in the South Pacific, circumstances which had prompted a popular campaign for Australia to fund the building of a new "Dreadnought" battleship to bolster the imperial fleet. The New Zealand Government agreed to a similar proposal, but Fisher had resisted the move in favour of building several smaller ships for a local navy. Sean Scalmer has gone so far as to argue that the Dreadnought issue was an important factor in bringing the fusion to fruition, but in the event, the plan was abandoned after a Naval and Military Conference held in London advised against it.[102] This latest inconsistency inspired somebody to pen a poem on "Some famous Josephs and one in particular":

> But all these Josephs, and some more, if any you can name,
> Beside a Joseph in my mind, are feeble, poor, and tame.
> What, pray, of Joseph Cook, or am I really very dense,
> There never was a Joseph like Our Minister of Defence.
> He started as a Labour man, and now is not at all.
> He once was a Protectionist, and now esteems it gall.
> He once, at least it's so alleged, wore anti-British shoes,
> But now he's quite Disraeli like, in his Imperial views.
> The question is, if Joseph's fixed, or will he change again;
> On what new thing will Joseph raise, a controversial Cain?
> In twenty years from now you may discover that he's then,
> A different man again, as though, in him were many men.[103]

Despite this exposure to satire, the decision would prove fully justified, as the Dreadnought plan was replaced with one for a new Australian Navy which Cook can lay claim to having founded. This involved the construction of a new fleet to operate independently of Britain, led by the flagship,

Indefatigable Class battlecruiser *HMAS Australia*, and also consisting of three Bristol Class unarmoured cruisers, six River Class destroyers, and three C Class submarines. The cost was to be an astonishing £3.695m, which serves as testament to the gravity of the strategic concerns.[104] A critic might point out that Cook's navy resembled Fisher's plan, but Cook's was much more substantial, "as different as infant and adult".[105] He had long argued that a navy should be prioritised above land forces as the cornerstone of Australia's security, and he can take credit for having done the work and insisting on the grand scale of the project. Indeed, Cook had to resist concerted attempts by the Treasurer John Forrest to restrain his departmental budget, while Labor opposed the loan necessary to fund the ships.[106]

On the other issue of compulsory training, which was introduced under Cook's 1909 *Defence Act*, there was a clearer contradiction of articulated principle, but he nonetheless spearheaded the growth of Australia's armed forces ahead of their first real test in the looming global conflict. Other achievements include establishing the Royal Military College at Duntroon, building factories to produce small arms and munitions, encouraging rifle clubs in the manner he had previously advocated, laying the earliest groundwork for an Australian Air Force by offering a £5000 prize for the design of a military aircraft, and escorting Lord Kitchener on an extensive tour of Australia aimed at reorganising and strengthening the nation's defences. Those that had no memory of Cook's time as a NSW Minister were actually quite shocked to find that he could be as successful at being constructive as he had been at opposing things.[107]

Beyond Cook's portfolio, the government's legislative record arguably suited the beliefs and interests of Cook's side of the fusion. The *Seat of Government Act* was finalised, a new Commonwealth-State financial agreement at last replaced the "Braddon Blot", and the pursuit of new protection was largely abandoned. Cook's working relationship with Deakin gradually moved from cautious, to productive, to actively friendly, as both men enjoyed the stability and downright relief that a two-party system ushered in. The spirit of cordiality was symbolised when the post of Australia's first High Commissioner in London was offered to George Reid, though Deakin could not bring himself to convey the news personally and instead sent Cook to do so. Reid was farewelled with a grand banquet in Sydney Town Hall, during which Cook toasted him as "my big brother".[108]

Cook was highly optimistic about the government's chances in the upcoming election, which for the first time would be a simple contest of Liberal versus Labor. There was a real positivity to his liberal vision which improved circumstances allowed to shine, and this was best demonstrated in a lecture he gave at the Lyceum Hall on the topic of "Is the world growing better?". This pointed out man's natural instinct to be pessimistic, quoting from Macaulay: "Have all my life been hearing of the decay of the nation, but seen nothing but signs of progress", before citing increases in life expectancy, reductions in crime, decreases in the cost of education, better housing, a more even distribution of wealth, improved communications technology and greater care for the aged, as evidence of a moral and material progress that had been produced by the expansion of freedom combined with "social discipline" and the acceptance of duty.[109] He also touched on one of the great ironies, which was that socialist ideas seemed only to be proposed in prosperous countries, where people had grown used to improvements, and were thus susceptible to propaganda which claimed they could be artificially sped up.

The election's end result of a decisive Labor victory undoubtedly came as a shock to Cook. This was the third consecutive election in which a Deakin-led party had lost a significant number of seats, suggesting that he had never been a vote-winner, but this was on a far bigger scale. Clearly supporters of both sides of the fiscal divide were unhappy about the compromises involved in the fusion, while local issues also played their part. Cook singled out the NSW Liberal Government's "unnecessarily severe" handling of a coal strike as something that served to really galvanise the Labor vote in his home State.[110] He noted that Labor's extra-parliamentary organisation remained streaks ahead of what the Liberals had achieved, despite his concerted efforts on that front, and he also lamented that Labor had successfully whipped up class feelings, believing that they "could not have a nation divided up without injury being done to its highest and truest interests".[111]

The Liberal Leader

Despite losing office, the Liberals left their leadership unchanged. Parliament was going through a transition phase; while the fusion had already created a significant degree of stabilisation, there were now few independent members left, and with the ascent of a caucus government that decided everything behind closed doors, debates were shorter and there was arguably less scrutiny of legislation, particularly as the Senate was proving itself to be more of a party House than a States' House.

If Parliament was less of a check and balance on the actions of the government, this heightened the importance of the High Court, but Fisher determined to minimise its role via constitutional referenda to greatly expand the powers of the Commonwealth. The people were to be asked to grant powers to legislate on "trade, commerce, the control of corporations, labour and employment, including wages and conditions; and the settling of disputes; and combinations and monopolies" (all controversially combined into a single referendum question), and separately to grant the power to nationalise monopolies.

In the ensuing lengthy campaign, Cook vigorously took up the fight against what he regarded as "unification" and an attempt to take out the "umpire" (the High Court).[112] He believed that Australia was too large a country to be ruled from one place; it had a diversity of problems that required diverse solutions. The Commonwealth had enough difficulty dealing with its existing responsibilities like defence such that getting it to control everything could only detract from its primary responsibilities. Balance was the strength of a federal system, but:

> Mr. Hughes proposes to pick up the dividing fence and carry it over on the State side until there is only a diminutive State paddock left alongside a large and spacious Federal one.[113]

Aiming his pitch at working men, Cook also pointed out that federal control of pay and conditions meant average control, and that since NSW workers were already some of the best treated they were likely to lose out, and he picked up the old argument that the Senate was undemocratic so giving more powers to the Commonwealth would give the people less direct control.[114] He was helped in this appeal by a split in Labor ranks whereby the newly-elected McGowen Government of NSW refused to support the proposals and its leaders were subject to recriminations from the AWU, which Cook seized upon as exactly the kind of trampling of free thought which he had warned that caucus involved. On the back of these cross-party concerns the referenda were easily defeated, with 'yes' receiving less than 40 per cent of the vote in both cases.

Beyond the strains of the campaign, this was a relatively relaxing period in Cook's life. The combination of the muted Parliament which sat less frequently and having a party leader based in Melbourne meant there was less need for constant travel, and Cook spent much of his time cultivating an orchard at Baulkham Hills which featured both citrus and stone-fruit trees.[115] The venture was a joint enterprise with one of his sons, and while it made only modest profit, it was a source of great contentment. While Joseph was taking it easy (by his standards at least), Mary was picking up the slack and becoming more politically active, for she was frequently to be found addressing meetings of the Women's Liberal League.

This peaceful state was not to last, as Deakin's increasing ill-health saw Cook take up an increasing burden of the work in the House, and then in January 1913 came the shock news that the fusion leader was retiring. Cook was astounded by this "bolt from the blue" and sought out Deakin's son-in-law to confirm if the decision was final.[116] It appears that Cook did not initially view this as his long-awaited opportunity, but rather a threat to the unity of a party that might easily dissolve back into its constituent parts.

That possibility loomed likely, as when the party met to elect a leader the vote split evenly and largely along fiscal lines. In the end Deakin had the casting vote, which he gave to Cook over the distinguished West Australian John Forrest. This was perhaps surprising, but it was Cook's tireless efforts and potential for future energetic action which had impressed him on his former adversary, who privately justified his decision in the following terms:

> [Cook's] services for 3 years as Deputy Leader unfaltering, honourable, untiring and capable have made his claim irresistible against Forrest who has been casual and neglectful in the House. Also because to pass Cook over now would be to brand him once and for all – Forrest is 65 has been seriously threatened by ill health and knows he cannot last. He wishes to take the post for a time having the honour and glory of retiring at leisure ... Greatly as I sympathise with him I acted solely in the interests of the party and its future as I see them.[117]

Cook's vitality was indeed a political imperative because he took the reins of the Liberal Party with just four months to go before the next election. That poll would be make or break for the fusion, and indeed the nature of Australia's political divide; in the meantime, the vast majority of protectionists resolved to hold their tongues about having a free trade-associated leader and see how it played out.

During the campaign Cook would speak in every State barring Western Australia, a gruelling schedule which once again sort to make manifest a national community in the manner of Reid's anti-socialist efforts.[118] Cook's task was made somewhat easier by the fact that the government had decided to double down on its commitment to enlarging Commonwealth powers, with six new referendum questions to be asked simultaneously with the general election. In such circumstances the "socialist tiger" was not the theoretical animal that Reid had had to contend with, it was entirely tangible, and Cook insisted that "socialism is the goal, unification is the means to reach it".[119] He took Labor's platform at face value, describing the socialist objective as "the principle that the state must become more and more omnipotent, until it eventually takes over all the actions of the individual, shaping and determining all our production, distribution and exchange".[120] Cook believed that Australia's existing economic system was "better than any other in the world to-day", and the constructive policy was to build upon it, not to take it apart root and branch in the naive hope that they might further outdo all of humanity.[121] In summary, "the Liberal Party stood for private enterprise consistent with the public interest".[122]

Beyond the referenda, one of the central electoral issues was a rapidly rising cost of living. This had a number of sources, including the high price of agricultural exports, the inflationary cycles associated with wage arbitration, and obviously the tariff. Cook did acknowledge the effect of the latter, but in prototypical Liberal fashion he latched on to the high burdens created by Labor's tax and spend policies, which he claimed had increased public expenditure by 52 per cent.[123] Despite the rising returns associated with the export boom, the government had completely outspent prosperity and was relying on new loans, which would have to be serviced, and money taken from the people's pockets. Every family was paying £8/5/ per year more in tax than three years ago, and Labor's new land tax had failed to break up land monopolies in the manner it promised but had done a great job in indirectly increasing rents when landowners inevitably passed on the cost. What would now be called productivity had also gone down, with 250 strikes in two years bringing industry to a standstill.[124]

Like Menzies' later claim that the Liberals were determined to be a progressive party, Cook's main policy speech delivered at Parramatta Town Hall associated liberalism with progress but insisted that progress succeeded most under conditions of freedom rather than the proposals offered by the "dazzling displays of political necromancers".[125] The Liberals' central positive policy was to open up immigration under the strategic imperative "that we must either people this continent or perish". They also proposed a "comprehensive scheme of national insurance, providing for sickness, accidents, maternity, widowhood, and unemployment, on a contributory basis, emphasising, again, that it is intended to be supplementary to the present pensions, and not in substitution for them". The contributory basis was central to how this fitted into a liberal philosophy, as it not only ensured such schemes could be financially sustainable, but also that people were not living off the charity of the state when it could be avoided, and that they thus maintained their independence and dignity. The comment on the pension reflected the fact that Labor had been conducting an early form of the "Mediscare", inciting fears that the Liberals would repeal pensions despite the fact that they were the ones who had introduced them.[126] Cook's speech concluded:

> Our ideal is that of a wise devolution and definition of national powers, the states continuing to develop within their present sovereignties their own internal resources; the federation in its sphere attending to its already ample obligations in matters of defence, territorial development, and external affairs; harmonious cooperation taking the place of the present friction and distrust; each assisting the power of the other to control, to defend, and to develop the immense resources of our wonderful continent; making it the home of millions of free, enlightened, and prosperous people, who, in turn, will preserve the traditions of the race, and hand them on to succeeding generations, honoured, respected, and unimpaired.

The pitch hit home, with the Liberals picking up a net gain of seven seats and all the referendum proposals going down, albeit far more narrowly than on the first attempt. Cook was the first Liberal and the first centre-right leader to win a majority in his own right, and he did it by advocating enduring liberal values that have continued to define his side of politics. The margin of victory could not have been slimmer, as the Liberals achieved just a one seat majority and would have to rely on the casting vote of the Speaker but considering all the obstacles to be overcome in transforming the divided fusion into an electable alternative government in a little over one hundred days, it was a tremendous achievement.

The one major drawback was the Senate, which was not yet elected on proportional representation, and thus allowed one party to win all the seats from a given State with any narrow majority. There the caucus would have complete veto over any legislation, and Cook was faced with the option of either enjoying office as a do-nothing government for three years or risking it all attempting to "crash through or crash".

Prime Minister

Throughout his political career, Cook had always found time for lay-preaching, and this remained true even after he had obtained the highest office in the land. Less than a week after being sworn in as prime minister he delivered an address to the Croydon Park Methodist Young Men's Union on the importance of tolerance and personal responsibility:

> You cannot have the brotherhood of man by preaching and practising the hatred of men whose opinions you differ from...[Y]ou cannot treat men just as you would a machine. Man is a thinking individual with a soul and a mind, as well as a body.

> In men, as in the rest of nature, there is an immense variety of types. No statesman, or anybody else, can set down one rule, and guarantee it as the prescription to cure all the ills of society... I know of but one remedy which can offer a cure for the body politic, and it is human character. Character is confidence; it is honesty; it is security. It is the one source from which is developed a higher and better personality. You may pass a hundred thousand laws, and create a better environment, but unless you create a better man he will soon make a mess of the environment... If you could get good personality and good character you would go a long way towards solving the problems of the unemployed, the cost of living, and everything else. If character is to be the only abiding basis for a healthy democracy, we should concentrate all our efforts on building up character.[127]

Cook was about to face his latest test of personal character. Reading Murdoch's biography, you get the impression of a man who had been too long in Opposition, who continued to fight rather than act in the conciliatory manner necessary in a prime minister (a Tony Abbott figure perhaps). But, as the *Argus* put it, Cook was "a man who feels deeply, and such a man scorns the arts of the time-server".[128] He was never going to be happy just collecting a prime ministerial salary, even though it was the highest he had ever earned; Cook was there to stand up for principles he deeply believed in.

That is not to say that there was much of a choice on offer.

When the House first met after the election, Labor made it clear that they would be as obstructionist and caustic as possible, immediately moving a censure motion and refusing to even allow the common courtesy of pairing absent members. In the ensuing session, seemingly non-contentious measures, transferring control of Norfolk Island to the Commonwealth, providing for the development of the Northern Territory, and establishing an Agricultural Bureau (a forerunner to the CSIRO which sought to build on Cook's achievements as a NSW Minister), would be treated by the Opposition with a considerable deal of hostility. In such circumstances, Cook resolved to test out the constitutional mechanism of the double dissolution, which had been specifically designed to resolve deadlocks between the two Houses. The only question was, on what issue should the battle be fought?

Cook picked out two, both of which had featured prominently in the recent election campaign. The first was postal voting, which the previous Labor government had abolished. Both sides had an element of self-interest in their positions on the issue, for at the time the stereotype was that postal votes were mainly utilised by rich women who did not want to deal with the riff-raff at the polling booth. However, for Cook this was a deeper issue about access to the franchise which touched multiple groups, and indeed he had been demanding and defending the concept of a postal vote since before he even left the

Labor Party.[129]

The other issue was one which epitomised how Cook's views had evolved over the years, and this was preference to unionists in government employment. This meant that whenever the government advertised a job and two men applied, the man who was a union member would be automatically favoured. This was a fundamental breach of equality and personal liberty, which was made all the worse because the unions had become so heavily politicised that paying a union fee was tantamount to making a donation to the Labor Party. Cook still believed that voluntary cooperation was a good thing for workers, but the element of compulsion in making a man's livelihood contingent on his affiliation was reminiscent of the pledge and a flagrant attack on moral independence, and he therefore sought to abolish the preference.

After Treasurer John Forrest delivered a budget which aimed to rein in spending in all areas other than defence (where it expanded in line with increasing global tensions), the two Bills were introduced on 31 October 1913, each containing only one operative clause to give Labor little room to stonewall. Nevertheless, the Opposition found innovative ways to try to avoid a double dissolution, with Senate Leader Gregor McGregor conducting a "strike" of repeated adjournment motions to avoid voting on the Bills. This could only be carried on so long, and eventually they were rejected, leaving the government to wait at least three months before resubmitting them in order to meet the necessary constitutional conditions.

Much of the ensuing parliamentary recess was spent preparing for the inevitable election, but there was also time to enjoy some of the fruits of office. There was considerable relief that an outbreak of smallpox had been brought under control; at one stage the situation had been so serious that there had even been talk of the need for compulsory vaccinations. The prime minister had dismissed this as a decision for the State governments, but much work had to go into developing adequate quarantine methods and facilities.[130]

With the threat alleviated, Cook got to view a baseball exhibition match between the New York Giants and the Chicago White Sox that attracted a roaring crowd to the SCG. He entertained High Commissioner Sir George Reid, who was home for a visit and who was given specific instructions on how to encourage immigration once he returned to England. Cook also visited Canberra to inspect the earliest stages of the construction of the new capital and while there managed to resolve a strike by offering ameliorative terms to the local workers.[131]

Parliament resumed in April 1914, and on 28 May the House of Representatives passed the Government Preference Prohibition Bill only for it to be immediately rejected by the Senate.[132] Cook promptly sought a double dissolution from the Governor General Sir Ronald Munro

Ferguson, who was fresh off the boat from England, and who had to consult with Chief Justice Samuel Griffith as there was no precedent for determining whether an issue was considerable enough to warrant the use of the mechanism. Labor complained about setting the precedent that the Senate could be threatened with a dissolution for not passing bills. It quixotically petitioned the Governor General to block the dissolution, or otherwise attach a third attempt at its desired constitutional referenda to the election (the Governor General had the power to grant referenda for constitutional amendments only approved by one House, another mechanism which had not yet been tried). This was refused on Cook's advice, as was a demand to publish the confidential memoranda that passed between the Crown's representative and the Ministry during this protracted process; but assent for Australia's first double dissolution was forthcoming.

Delivering his main policy speech on 14 July, Cook framed the election as a battle for the maintenance of responsible government, which had been threatened by Labor's obstructionist Senate and submission to an external caucus.[133] He sought to facilitate a healthier Australian democracy via proposals to introduce proportional voting for the Senate, preferential voting for the House of Representatives, restore the postal vote, remove unreasonable press restrictions, introduce uniform electoral rolls for State and Federal elections, and improve electoral machinery and safeguards.

Beyond this, the speech had a notable rural emphasis that presaged the emergence of the Country Party, which Cook was actively trying to forestall. He alluded to the rich agricultural history of the Parramatta district:

> Here, where the first crops were grown and reaped, is surely the place from which to propound a policy vibrating with sympathy for the grain growers and cultivators of today. Here, too, where the first flax factory and the first Australian woollen mills still stand, is the place from which appropriately to emphasise the priceless value to the nation of its industrial operators and the absolute necessity for leaving them reasonably alone in their callings, and freeing them from all unnecessary and irritating interference, as well as encouraging them in all wise ways.

In response to farmers' concerns about a beef trust which had been exposed in Brisbane, Cook affirmed that he would support some enlargement of the Commonwealth's powers to deal with the issue, provided this were done in a manner that would not undermine federalism like the Labor proposals. Such back-tracking did not augur well, but other aspects of this appeal to rural voters fitted naturally within Cook's existing policy framework, namely decentralisation, the Agricultural Bureau, and the development of inland Australia which would take the bulk of a new wave of migration. It was enough to win endorsement from the Farmers and Settlers' Association and successfully delay the splintering of the centre-right into what is now the Coalition.[134]

What the outcome of an election fought on this basis would have been we will never know, because a month out from the poll the First World War broke out and the entire discourse shifted. Bowing to the wishes of Ferguson, Cook had to cut short his election campaign to focus on military preparations, spending four weeks cooped up in his office when he would normally have been out touring the nation. In such circumstances, Labor benefitted from both the comparatively light burdens of Opposition, and also the fact that it had its strong union organisation to fall back on. Nor did it help that Cook had essentially put his foot in his mouth by complaining about the extravagance of specific aspects of Labor's defence spending shortly before war was declared.

A proposal to postpone the election was raised but Cook ultimately decided against this as reconstituting a dissolved Parliament would have been a constitutional nightmare.[135] An act of the Imperial Parliament could theoretically have achieved the result if desired, but Cook felt this would undermine Australia's rights as a self-governing dominion. Fisher opportunistically exploited this decision, accusing the prime minister of refusing a political truce and deliberately keeping party strife alive.

While there was much debate on whether to hold elections, there could be no question about the general thrust of the government's response to news of war. Australia automatically joined in along with Great Britain and Cook offered an initial expeditionary force of 20,000 men, while moves were rapidly made to seize German wireless installations in the Pacific. As a deeply religious man, the military commitment lay heavily on Cook's conscience. Three of his sons would end up enlisting, and 'Sid' would be twice wounded at Gallipoli including suffering a bullet to the head, though remarkably they would all survive.[136] Despite his strong belief in Empire, Cook had no jingoistic enthusiasm for the conflict and unlike many predicted from the outset that it would be a long and grim fight, even if he determined that it was ultimately a necessary one. The manifesto he issued at the end of the election campaign warned the nation to:

> Remember that the war has only just begun. It unhappily bids fair to last long. It may be both costly and ghostly and levy heavy toll not only of precious lives but also on the resources of the country. But whatever the sacrifices may be, it must be prosecuted to the bitter end, if need be, for our lives and liberties are in the issue, and the national destiny is in the scale. If money is needed it must be provided - our country has grown rich under Imperial protection. If more men are wanted, they, too, will be forthcoming. The war must go on until the reign of peace "with freedom full and fair" is again set up throughout our Western civilisation.[137]

The political and emotional burden of leading the nation through such an ordeal was avoided by the result of the election, which saw the Liberals lose six seats by narrow margins and Labor thus return to power with a comfortable majority. The Liberals did better than in 1910 under Deakin, both in terms of losses and the overall number of votes received, but the crucible of war would soon see the abandonment of the debate over freedom and the role of the state which the party represented. Cook's last statement before resigning as prime minister was used to express his deepest sympathy to the relatives of Australian soldiers who had been killed in the fight to capture the island of New Britain (now remembered as the Battle of Bita Paka).[138]

The War and Afterwards

Cook was sanguine about the election result, telling a party of well-wishers "office at my time of life does not concern me one bit. I have come to the point of life when only one thing concerns me, and that is this: I wish to do my duty to Australia (loud cheers)".[139] He promised as Leader of the Opposition to give full support to the government in pursuing the war effort, but also noted that he would continue to oppose any partisan legislation that might distract from it. Through much of 1915 partisan division did indeed seem likely to boil-over, as Labor pushed for a fresh batch of constitutional referenda, but Cook's sustained objection to conducting them during wartime ultimately saw them postponed.

Otherwise, Cook's vast energy was poured into multiple recruiting campaigns. He was utterly convinced that the war needed to be won in order to preserve freedom, democracy and ultimately Australia against the forces of military autocracy, and by mid-1916 he was coming around to the view that the voluntary principle might have to be abandoned in favour of conscription. This was no easy decision for him, he detested compulsion and was certainly not in the vanguard with the earliest proponents of the proposal. The wounded Sid returned home at this time, so Cook can have been under no illusions as to what he would be forcing men into, but he ultimately judged that "manhood suffrage denoted manhood responsibility".[140]

The conclusion that the liberty of the present needed to be sacrificed in order to preserve liberty's future prospects also informed Cook's attitude towards parliamentary government. There was no figure in his entire career whom Cook had clashed with more frequently or more fervently than the man who had replaced Fisher as prime minister in October 1915, William Morris Hughes – or as Cook preferred to call him "that little devil".[141] But personal issues were entirely trivial at this point, and so it was that when the Labor Party was split violently asunder by the conscription issue, Cook would lend his support to the embattled Labor Leader. Cook played a central role in how the whole affair played out; for if he had come out in favour of conscription earlier Labor would likely have closed ranks and treated it as a party issue.[142] His own hesitation gave Hughes time in office to get to grips with the gravity of the situation and be seen as making up his own mind.

Following the first plebiscite on conscription, which was narrowly defeated, Hughes was expelled from the Labor Party along with a sizeable following, and Caucus Labor moved a motion of censure against the prime minister, which the Liberals voted against. It would still be some time before the Liberals agreed to form a coalition government, initially guaranteeing confidence and supply only. Some Deakinites within the party were quite ready to accept Hughes' views in favour of an interventionist state, while Cook had significant motivation to try to keep the flame of liberalism alive.[143] However eventually terms were hammered out under the urging of the Governor General and the imperative that the prime minister be given the security to attend an Imperial Conference in London to discuss vital war matters. Hughes would remain the head of government, the Liberals would get six of eleven Cabinet positions, and both parties agreed to a free vote on tax policy.

In the new "Hughes-Cook" Ministry, the Liberal Leader was sworn in as Minister for the Navy, putting his ego aside in allowing the existing Defence Minister hold on to his position. Caucus Labor still had the numbers in the Senate, but an election was forthcoming, and this consummated the Ministry's fusion into a new Nationalist Party. A sweeping victory helped to mask a bitter fact: the

Liberal Party had ceased to exist and would not re-emerge until the dying stages of the next war.

Cook spent the rest of 1917 dealing with striking maritime workers and campaigning for the second conscription plebiscite. By the end of the year his characteristic boundless energy was finally starting to fail him. He openly admitted that he was tired and somewhat sick of office, but some excitement and relief was to come in 1918, for Cook was asked to travel to England to join Hughes in representing Australia at a new Imperial Conference. After more than 30 years, he was to return to the land of his birth.

The party travelled via America, with Cook able to marvel at Seattle's huge ship-building enterprises, before stopping over in New York and Washington to meet with officials in the Woodrow Wilson administration. In England, Cook's trip involved several triumphal moments. He met the King several times, and was ultimately knighted in the Order of St. Michael and St. George, the culmination of his social rise which the *Sydney Morning Herald* lauded as "a striking example of the opportunities offered to all citizens of a free democracy".[144] As "Sir Joe", he then conducted a procession through his native Silverdale, and was given the freedom of the local Borough of Newcastle-under-Lyme, an occasion on which he took the opportunity reiterate his strong belief in subsidiarity: "Is it not the very essence of the democratic instinct that the nearer you can take the government to the people of the country the more certain it is that it is better controlled and the more wisely it is ordained, the more certain it is also that the more economically it is administered".[145]

But, being wartime, there were also many sombre moments. Cook visited large numbers of injured Australian troops recovering in various hospitals, he took a trip to the front at Bellecourt where he got so close to the action that shell explosions splashed his face with mud, and he served as a pall-bearer at Reid's funeral.

Cook still did get not along very well with Hughes, and over the months spent in common purpose they became so estranged that the issue was brought up in the House of Representatives as a matter impacting on the public interest.[146] Nevertheless, as they were still in England when the guns fell silent, Cook and Hughes both accompanied the British delegation to the Paris Peace Conference. There Cook's thoughtful contribution was largely overshadowed by his bombastic chief, though David Lloyd George did take note of Cook as one of the "fervent believers" in both the desirability and feasibility of the League of Nations and described him as 'a man of calm and balanced judgement' (very much contrasting with Hughes).[147] Cook did make a notable impact in one unlikely area. Somehow, he became the British representative on a committee in charge of determining the borders of Czechoslovakia, despite self-evidently having limited knowledge of the subject. He voted to enlarge them at the expense of Germany (thereby helping to set the scene for Hitler's later annexation).

Cook was an official signatory of the Treaty of Versailles, for which he had to provide a family seal which was reported to feature a sea lion riding on waves.[148] He optimistically described the document as a "new Magna Charta", likely being unaware that King John and the Barons were quickly back at war with each other after the signing of the first one.[149]

After 16 months abroad, Cook finally arrived home in late August 1919. By this stage, the rumour was that he had his eyes set on retirement and particularly the post of High Commissioner that was soon to be vacated by Fisher. Hughes had taken all the credit for their joint efforts in England and France, and Cook was put in a position where he had to withdraw from the Nationalists' deputy leadership to allow it to fall to William Watt, the acting prime minister for over a year, only for Watt to refuse the offer.

Though Cook might have been emotionally done with party politics, he essentially had to remain if he wanted to guarantee himself the diplomatic posting. He fought the 1919 election, giving half-hearted endorsement to the postponed referenda that Hughes insisted on carrying out and trying once again to ameliorate an attempt to directly represent farming interests in the Parliament. This time the emergence of the Country Party could not be forestalled, particularly as it acted as an outlet for centre-right voters to vent their frustrations over Hughes' Labor-light approach.

This was to curse Cook, as the Nationalists were left without their own majority and he had to stick around to lend strength to the Ministry. He even got roped into becoming Treasurer, delivering two deflationary budgets which concentrated on curtailing spending.[150] These pleased few people, and Cook was subject to bitter criticism, but he got his reward in the form of the High Commissionership and spent several years happily fighting to attract immigrants and British investment during the Bruce-Page era when such things were central to the government's national development agenda.

Given his own remarkable story, Cook was ideally suited to selling Australia as "The Land of the Better Chance" to potential migrants, and during his tenure in London Australia's net overseas migration was maintained at the most consistently high levels seen between federation and the post-war boom that would kick in from 1948.[151] Cook was responsible for raising government loans, and managed to successfully negotiate the first ever Commonwealth loan of US dollars from New York when the Bank of England became concerned about excessive sterling foreign loans undermining their gold standard.[152] On the whole, Cook was largely supportive of Bruce's borrowing program (not that he could maintain a personal stance). However, he did take issue with the system of running up large overdrafts with the Westminister and Commonwealth banks which would come back to bite the nation in the Great Depression.

Even with the plum posting, Cook remained as concerned about taking money off the people as ever, and he therefore led a major retrenchment in the bloated staff of Australia House conducted in the interests of the taxpayer. Despite this pairing back, Australia House became "one of the busiest spots in London", simultaneously serving as a commercial hub and a tourist attraction with visitors' books signed by thousands of people each year. Of all his duties, Cook took particular delight in arranging Australia's contribution to the Great Empire Exhibition staged in Wembley in 1924 and 1925 which saw 17 million people attend the first year alone.[153] Australia's section covered five acres, and was essentially a giant advertisement for antipodean produce. Cook was especially pleased with the "King's Christmas pudding in which all Dominions were represented" and in which the Australian fruit he had long prized took a starring role.

As High Commissioner, Cook became involved in important foreign policy matters, acting as Australia's chief delegate to the League of Nations in Geneva for several years. He broke ranks with Britain to urge the League to intervene in the Chanak crisis, vigorously defended Australia's administration of the mandated territories of New Guinea and Nauru and made some remarks about the admission of Abyssinia into the League that a decade later would be quoted by Baron Aloisi, representative of the Mussolini regime, to justify Italy's interventions in Africa. The latter caused quite a storm and prompted Cook to suggest that Britain and the League's members had a duty to protect Abyssinia in a move that would have ended "appeasement" before it started.[154] While he made some waves in Geneva, in London Cook's influence as an Australian voice on British foreign policy was less significant than it may otherwise have been, as Bruce undercut him by appointing a young Richard Casey as Australian Liaison Officer with the Foreign Office "to be considered as his mouthpiece and representative on all matters of foreign policy". Bruce wanted his Commissioner to be an insider to both Whitehall and Westminster, but he did not believe that Cook had the necessary skill-set "notwithstanding the fact that he has many excellent qualities", and this perhaps reflected a prejudice against his humble origins (either on the part of Bruce or the London establishment). Nevertheless, Cook's success on the marketing front meant that when he finally left Britain "Australia's stock stood higher than that of any other Dominion".

Returning home in 1927, Cook survived another twenty years and got to see the re-emergence of a party dedicated to the tenets of a uniquely Australian centre-right liberalism for which he had fought and helped to define. By all accounts he lived out his days with the quiet satisfaction of a man who had worked hard and done his duty.[155] He had simultaneously lived up to and defied his father's epitaph, earning his rest in both this life and the next.

Endnotes

1 John Murdoch, *Sir Joe: A political biography of Sir Joseph Cook*, Minerva Press, London, 1996, p.xii.

2 G. Bebbington, *Pit Boy to Prime Minister: The story of the Rt. Hon. Sir Joseph Cook, P.C., G.C.M.G.*, Centre of Local & Community History, Keele, 1988, p. 1.

3 Ibid., p.8.

4 M.H. Ellis, "Joseph Cook: The incredible Prime Minister", *The Bulletin*, 10 November 1962, p. 20.

5 Murdoch, *Sir Joe: a political biography of Sir Joseph Cook*, pp.16-7.

6 Bebbington, *Pit Boy to Prime Minister*, p. 14.

7 Murdoch, *Sir Joe: A political biography of Sir Joseph Cook*, p. 24.

8 "Shot-Firing in Mines", *Glen Innes Examiner and General Advertiser*, 24 May 1887, p. 2.

9 'Lithgow Miners' Demonstration', *Daily Telegraph*, 4 July 1887, p.4, "Anti-Chinese Meeting at Lithgow", *Sydney Morning Herald*, 29 February 1888, p.7, "The Lithgow Water Reserve", *Sydney Morning Herald*, 8 December 1888, p.11, "Lithgow Thursday", *Sydney Morning Herald*, 22 June 1888, p.8, and 'The Unemployed at Lithgow', *Sydney Morning Herald*, 17 April 1889, p. 7.

10 "Lithgow", *Bathurst Free Press and Mining Journal*, 21 July 1890, p.3.

11 L.G. Churchward, "The American Influence on the Australian Labour Movement", *Historical Studies: Australia and New Zealand*, Vol. 5, No. 19, November 1952, pp. 258-77.

12 Henry George, *Progress and Poverty: An Inquiry into the Cause of Industrial Depressions and of Increase of Want with Increase of Wealth: The Remedy*, D. Appleton, New York, 1879.

13 Ibid., p. 364.

14 "Addresses by Labour Members", *Wagga Wagga Express*, 3 May 1894, p. 4.

15 Henry George, *Protection or Free Trade: An Examination of the Tariff Question with Especial Regard to the Interests of Labour*, Kegan Paul, Trench, London, 1890, pp. 50-60.

16 Ellis, "Joseph Cook: The incredible Prime Minister", p. 20.

17 'The Coalminers' Strike', *Sydney Morning Herald*, 11 November 1990, p. 3.

18 *Report of the Royal Commission on Strikes*, Government Printer, Sydney, 1891, p. 324.

19 Murdoch, *Sir Joe: A political biography of Sir Joseph Cook*, p. 34.

20 "Lithgow Friday", *Sydney Morning Herald*, 13 June 1891, p. 7.

21 "Hartley Election", *Katoomba Times*, 20 June 1891, p. 2.

22 'Lithgow Monday', *Sydney Morning Herald*, 17 June 1891, p .8.

23 'Mr. Joseph Cook", *Daily Telegraph*, 30 June 1891, p. 3.

24 'Hartley', *Sydney Morning Herald*, 22 June 1891, p. 5.

25 "Political Notes", *Evening News*, 23 June 1891, p. 5.

26 "One of Them", *The Bulletin*, 18 March 1893, pp. 6-7.

27 Bede Nairn, *Civilising Capitalism: The Labor Movement in New South Wales 1870-1900*, Australian National University Press, Canberra, 1973, p. 67.

28 bid., p.7 4.

29 Zachary Gorman, "A Contested Contest: George Reid's election to the leadership of the New South Wales Free Trade Party", *Journal of Australian Colonial History*, Vol. 18, July 2016, pp. 182-197.

30 "Messrs. Cook and Donald at Katoomba South", *Katoomba Times*, 10 June 1892, p. 4.

31 "Mr. Cook MP at Broken Hill", *Illawarra Mercury*, 1 November, 1892, p. 3.

32 Nairn, *Civilising Capitalism*, p. 93.

33 "The Parliamentary Labor Party", *Daily Telegraph*, 21 April 1894, p. 11.

34 Judith Brett, *Australian Liberals and the Moral Middle Class: From Alfred Deakin to John Howard*, Cambridge University Press, Cambridge, 2003, pp. 17-41.

35 Cook had some guilt by association on the sectarian front, but even the *Catholic Press* ultimately admitted that he did not fan the issue, "After the Battle", *Catholic Press*, 5 June 1913, p. 31.

36 Antony Green, *New South Wales Election Results 1856-2007*, Parliament of New South Wales, Sydney, 2007.

37 "After the Polling", *Daily Telegraph*, 20 July 1894, p. 5.

38 "The Proposed Land Tax", *Freeman's Journal*, 21 July 1894 p. 10.

39 "The Political Situation", *Sydney Morning Herald*, 3 August 1894, p. 5.

40 W.G. McMinn, *George Reid*, Melbourne University Press, Carlton, 1989, p. 93.

41 'Hartley', *Daily Telegraph*, 13 August 1894, p. 5.

42 Murdoch, *Sir Joe: A political biography of Sir Joseph Cook*, p. 49.

43 Bebbington, *Pit Boy to Prime Minister*, p. 28.

44 Murdoch, *Sir Joe: A political biography of Sir Joseph Cook*, throughout.

45 "Death of Sir George Reid", *Sydney Morning Herald*, 13 September 1918, p. 6.

46 'Death of Sir George Reid', *Anzac Bulletin: issued to members of the Australian Imperial Forces in Great Britain and France by authority of the High Commissioner for Australia*, Issue 89, p. 12.

47 George Reid, *My Reminiscences*, Cassell, London, 1917.

48 McMinn, *George Reid*, 1989.

49 "Mr. Joseph Cook at Lithgow", *Daily Telegraph*, 16 May 1898, p .5.

50 "The Rough Total", *Sydney Morning Herald*, 6 June 1898, p. 5.

51 Zachary Gorman, "Birthplace of a nation?: Why Sydney voted no to federation", *Agenda: A Journal of Policy Analysis and Reform*, Vol. 27, Issue 1, pp. 125-48.

52 "The Postmaster-General at Lithgow", *Sydney Morning Herald*, 11 July 1898, p. 6.

53 "Mr. Joseph Cook", *Daily Telegraph*, 17 May 1899, p. 5.

54 Kevin Livingston, "Joseph Cook's Contribution", *Papers on Parliament*, No. 32, December 1998.

55 Murdoch, *Sir Joe: A political biography of Sir Joseph Cook*, p. 54.

56 H.V. Evatt, *Australian Labour Leader: The story of W. A. Holman and the Labour movement*, Angus and Robertson, Sydney, 1940, pp. 84-5.

57 Joseph Carruthers, "Motion of Censure", *NSW Parliamentary Debates*, 7 September 1899, p. 1273.

58 "Adult Suffrage Meeting at Auburn", Granville Independent and Parramatta Advertiser, 21 September 1900, p. 3.

59 "Mr. Joseph Cook at Penrith", *Nepean Times*, 23 February 1901, p. 3.

60 "The Commonwealth Elections", *Granville Independent and Parramatta Advertiser*, 16 February 1901, p. 6. It is worth mentioning that Sandford's ADB entry support's Cook's claim, suggesting that he installed a new steel furnace specifically because he was convinced that federation would lead to protection, John Perkins, 'Sandford, William (1841–1932)', *Australian Dictionary of Bi-*

ography, National Centre of Biography, Canberra, 1988.

61 "Federal Election", *Windsor and Richmond Gazette*, 2 March 1901, p. 6.

62 "The Federal Elections", *Nepean Times*, 6 April 1901, p. 6.

63 Outside of caucus, party affiliations were somewhat loose in the first term and there were also a number of 'Free Traders' committed to revenue tariffs, so these numbers should be viewed as approximate.

64 "Picnic to Mr. G.H. Reid", *Sydney Morning Herald*, 29 April 1901, p. 5.

65 Joseph Cook, "Governor General's Speech", *Commonwealth Parliamentary Debates*, House of Representatives, 22 May 1901, p. 169.

66 "The Commonwealth Parliament", *Sydney Morning Herald*, 1 November 1901, p. 6.

67 "Mr. Reid's Right Hand", *The Cumberland Argus and Fruitgrowers Advocate*, 2 October 1901, p. 2, "In the Federal Session", *Daily Telegraph*, 29 November 1901, p. 4.

68 "Anti-Tariff Demonstration", *Windsor and Richmond Gazette*, 30 November 1901, p. 1.

69 'The Duty on Boots", *The Cumberland Argus and Fruitgrowers Advocate*, 19 March 1902, p. 2.

70 "Esbank Iron and Steel Works", *The Australian Star*, 23 June 1902, p. 6.

71 Joseph Cook, "Defence Bill', *Commonwealth Parliamentary Debates*, House of Representatives, 5 August 1903.

72 "Our Telephone", *Sunday Times*, 9 August 1903, p. 2., "The Ballad of Blithesome Bill", *Sunday Times*, 30 August 1903, p.1.

73 "Our Federal Representatives", *The Cumberland Argus and Fruitgrowers Advocate*, 3 November 1903, p. 2.

74 "To the Editor", *Daily Telegraph*, 24 August 1903, p. 6.

75 "The Federal Elections", *Lithgow Mercury*, 3 November 1903, p. 5; "Politics by Day", *Evening News*, 13 November 1903, p. 5.

76 "Federal Election", *Windsor and Richmond Gazette*, 26 December 1903, p. 10.

77 "Our Federal Members", *The Cumberland Argus and Fruitgrowers Advocate*, 27 February 1904, p.4.

78 Joseph Cook, "Italian Immigration to Western Australia", *Com-*

monwealth Parliamentary Debates, House of Representatives, 21 April 1904.

79 "Federal Situation", *Sydney Morning Herald*, 18 April 1904 p. 6.

80 Joseph Cook, "Conciliation and Arbitration Bill", *Commonwealth Parliamentary Debates*, House of Representatives, 12 August 1904.

81 Billy Hughes, "Conciliation and Arbitration Bill", *Commonwealth Parliamentary Debates*, House of Representatives 12 August 1904.

82 "Political", *The Cumberland Argus and Fruitgrowers Advocate*, 20 August 1904, p. 4; "Mr. Reid and Mr. Coo"", *The Cumberland Argus and Fruitgrowers Advocate*, 24 August 1904, p. 2.

83 Zachary Gorman, *Sir Joseph Carruthers: Founder of the New South Wales Liberal Party*, Connor Court Publishing, Redland Bay, 2018.

84 Zachary Gorman, "George Reid's Anti-Socialist Campaign in the Evolution of Australian Liberalism", in Gregory Melleuish, *Liberalism and Conservatism*, Connor Court Publishing, Ballarat, 2016, pp. 17-38.

85 Joseph Cook, "Motion of Want of Confidence", *Commonwealth Parliamentary Debates*, House of Representatives 21 September 1904.

86 In a speech at Albury he quoted directly from Burke on how political beliefs like socialism could beget all the dogma and fanaticism of religion: "Socialistic Humbug", *Daily Telegraph*, 29 June 1905, p. 7.

87 "To Fight Socialism", *Daily Telegraph*, 18 May 1905, p. 5.

88 "The Liberal Party's Duty", *Daily Telegraph*, 9 March 1905, p. 5; "Mr. Joseph Cook in reply to Mr. Watson", *Sydney Morning Herald*, 21 April 1905, p. 9.

89 Joseph Cook, "Address-in-Reply", *Commonwealth Parliamentary Debates*, House of Representatives, 30 June 1905.

90 "Federal Politics", *Sydney Morning Herald*, 15 July 1905, p. 11.

91 George Reid, *My Reminiscences*, Cassell, London, 1917.

92 Frustratingly, the original article seems not to have survived and only extracts used by critics attest to its existence: "A Political Resurrection", *People*, 9 September 1905, p. 3.

93 "Mr. Watson and Mr. Winston Churchill", *Sydney Morning Herald*, 4 December 1906, p. 4.

94 C.A. Hughes and B.D. Graham, *A Handbook of Australian Government and Politics 1890-1964*, Australian National University, Can-

berra, 1968, p. 297. That result was with two NSW Anti-Socialist seats going uncontested, which likely hurt the party's Senate tally.

95 "Mr. Joseph Cook's Intention", *Sydney Morning Herald*, 26 August 1907, p. 8.

96 "After the Session", *Daily Telegraph*, 16 December 1907, p. 7.

97 J.A. La Nauze, *Alfred Deakin: A Biography Volume 2*, Melbourne University Press, Melbourne, 1965, pp.4, 35-8. One of Deakin's reasons for opposing the anti-socialist campaign had been that he believed socialism could not legally be carried out by the Commonwealth Government.

98 Joseph Cook, "Address-in-Reply', *Commonwealth Parliamentary Debates*, House of Representatives 17 September 1908.

99 "Mr. Reid's Statement", *Daily Telegraph*, 2 October 1908, p. 7.

100 For reasons of space, the fusion issue is dealt with in brief. For longer analysis see P. Loveday, A.W. Martin and R.S. Parker, *The Emergence of the Australian Party System*, Hale & Iremonger, Sydney, 1977; and Paul Strangio and Nick Dyrenfurth, *Confusion: The making of the Australian two-party system*, Melbourne University Press, Carlton, 2009.

101 Use of the term "Deakin-Cook" was widespread but far from universal. It recalled the Reid-McLean Government, which had been a coalition, hence "Deakin Ministry" was often used as being more appropriate to a single party.

102 Sean Scalmer, "For the sake of a straight out fight: The Free Traders and the Puzzle of the Fusion", in Strangio and Dyrenfurth, *Confusion: The making of the Australian two-party system*, pp. 45-69.

103 "Some Famous Josephs", *Clarence and Richmond Examiner*, 15 June 1909, p. 3.

104 Glenn Kerr, "The Decline of Australian Naval Deterrence 1919-1939", Royal Australian Navy, Canberra.

105 'Naval Defence', *Sunday Times*, 5 September 1909, p. 7.

106 Murdoch, *Sir Joe: A political biography of Sir Joseph Cook*, pp.83-4. David Kemp, *A Democratic Nation: Identity, Freedom and Equality in Australia 1901–1925*, Miegunyah Press, Carlton, 2019.

107 "Political", *The Cumberland Argus and Fruitgrowers Advocate*, 2 October 1909, p. 4.

108 "Sydney's Farewell", *Evening News*, 21 January 1910, p. 8.

109 "Is the world growing better?", *Daily Telegraph*, 7 March 1910, p. 9.

110 "Mr. Joseph Cook on the Fusion Rout", *Barrier Miner*, 16 April 1910, p. 4.

111 "The Elections", *Sydney Morning Herald*, 27 April 1910, p. 10.

112 "The Referenda", *The Cumberland Argus and Fruitgrowers Advocate*, 15 February 1911, p. 2.

113 "Echoes from the Arena", *Daily Telegraph*, 17 April 1911, p. 7.

114 "Surrendering Our Powers", *Daily Telegraph*, 17 March 1911, p. 8.

115 "Our Federal Member", *The Gosford Times and Wyong District Advocate*, 15 September 1911, p. 19.

116 La Nauze, *Alfred Deakin: A Biography Volume 2*, p. 623.

117 Ibid., p. 626.

118 "The Elections", *Sydney Morning Herald*, 11 April 1913, p. 10.

119 "Liberalism', *Sydney Morning Herald*, 4 April 1913, p. 6.

120 'Liberal Appeal", *Sydney Morning Herald*, 24 May 1913, p. 17.

121 "The Social Problem", *Sydney Morning Herald*, 28 May 1913, p. 14.

122 "The Liberal Leader", *Daily Telegraph*, 6 June 1913, p. 10.

123 "Condemned', *The Bathurst Times*, 29 March 1913, p. 2.

124 "Labour Tyranny", *Sydney Morning Herald*, 3 April 1913, p. 10.

125 Robert Menzies, *Afternoon Light: Some Memories of Men and Events*, Cassell, London, 1967, p. 286; "Liberalism", *Sydney Morning Herald*, 4 April 1913, p. 6.

126 "Old-Age Pensions", *Sydney Morning Herald*, 17 May 1913, p. 19.

127 "Problems of Life", *Sydney Morning Herald*, 10 June 1913, p. 8.

128 "Wednesday", *The Argus*, 15 June 1913, p. 12.

129 "Trades and Labour Council and Parliament", *Sydney Morning Herald*, 24 May 1894, p. 6.

130 "Mr. Cook in Sydney", *Evening News*, 18 July 1913, p. 7.

131 "Canberra Strike"' *Queanbeyan Age*, 10 February 1914, p. 3.

132 The summary account of this paragraph is based on Murdoch, *Sir Joe: A political biography of Sir Joseph Cook*, pp. 97-102.

133 "For Freedom", *Sydney Morning Herald*, 16 July 1914, p. 12.

134 "Farmers Will Support Liberals", *Sydney Morning Herald*, 16 July 1914, p. 9.

135 "Mr. Cook's Manifesto", *Daily Telegraph*, 17 August 1914, p. 6.

136 “Sid Cook Again Wounded”, *The Cumberland Argus and Fruitgrowers Advocate*, 18 August 1915, p. 2.

137 “Liberal Policy”, *Sydney Morning Herald*, 31 August 1914, p. 5.

138 “New Britain Fight”, *The Sun*, 15 September 1914, p. 5.

139 “Liberal Party”, *Sydney Morning Herald*, 3 October 1914, p. 14.

140 “Mighty Effort”, *Sunday Times*, 18 June 1916, p. 1.

141 Ellis, “Joseph Cook: The incredible Prime Minister”, p. 22.

142 Murdoch, *Sir Joe: A political biography of Sir Joseph Cook*, p. 113.

143 Kemp, *A Democratic Nation: Identity, Freedom and Equality in Australia 1901–1925*.

144 “Honoured by the King”, *Sydney Morning Herald*, 5 August 1918, p. 8.

145 Bebbington, *Pit Boy to Prime Minister*, p. 63.

146 James Boyd, “Sir Joseph Cook and the Prime Minister”, *Australian Parliamentary Debates*, 19 November 1918.

147 David Lloyd George, *The Truth About Peace Treaties*, Victor Gollancz, London, 1938, p. 631.

148 “Peace!”, *Dubbo Dispatch and Wellington Independent*, 1 July 1919, p. 1.

149 “A New Magna Charta”, *Sydney Morning Herald*, 3 July 1919, p. 7.

150 John Hawkins, “Joseph Cook: The reluctant treasurer”, *Economic Roundup*, Department of Treasury, Canberra, 2009.

151 Janet Phillips and Joanne Simon-Davies, “Migration to Australia: A quick guide to the statistics”, Parliamentary Library Research Paper Series, Commonwealth Parliament. Canberra.

152 Bernard Paul Attard, “The Australian High Commissioner’s Office Politics and Anglo-Australian Relations, 1901-1939”, PhD Thesis, St Antony’s College Oxford 1991.

153 Bernard Attard, “The high commissioners, empire development and economic diplomacy between the wars”, in Carl Bridge, Frank Bongiorno and David Lee, *The High Commissioners: Australia’s Representatives in the United Kingdom, 1910-2010*, Department of Foreign Affairs and Trade, Canberra, 2010.

154 “Abyssinia”, *Sydney Morning Herald*, 2 November 1935, p. 15.

155 F.K. Crowley, “Cook, Sir Joseph (1860–1947)”, *Australian Dictionary of Biography*, National Centre of Biography, Australian National University, Canberra, 1981.

www.ingramcontent.com/pod-product-compliance
Lightning Source LLC
La Vergne TN
LVHW010105110826
845155LV00028B/498

9781922815507